21 thine offspring shalt be in a million extracurricular activities 22 thou shalt not let them see you car dancing 23 thou shalt not wear thy wedding dress after thy wedding day 24 thou shalt be realistic 25 thou shalt not make a mess 26 thou shalt reserve thy fine china for special occasions 27 thou shalt hide thy weirdness 28 thou shalt not bring bananas on thy fishing boat 29 thou shalt get thine inbox to zero 30 thou shalt not swap sides of the bed 31 thou shalt be careful 32 only young children and high school seniors shalt take cheesy photos for oversize numbers 33 thou shalt not play hooky 34 thou shalt get a job with benefits 35 thou shalt not wear pajamas in public 36 thou shalt not draw on thy children 37 thou shalt not be ridiculous 38 thou shalt make thy bed 39 thou shalt care what other people think 40 thou shalt wait for permission #notarule

penguins can't fly

penguins can't fly

+39 other rules that don't exist

JASON KOTECKI

st. martin's griffin
new york

www.stmartins.com

Library of Congress Cataloging-in-Publication Data available upon request.

ISBN 978-1-250-06710-4 (paper over board)

ISBN 978-1-4668-7827-3 (e-book)

St. Martin's Griffin books may be purchased for educational, business, or promotional use. For information on bulk purchases, please contact the Macmillan Corporate and Premium Sales Department at 1-800-221-7945, extension 5442, or write to specialmarkets@macmillan.com.

First Edition: June 2015

10 9 8 7 6 5 4 3 2 1

[The images depicted in this book are not endorsed, sponsored, or affiliated with any toy or food products owners. Also, although no penguins were harmed in the making of this book, Adultitis took a good, swift kick in the pants.]

for mAry

iT'S TiMe TO DREAM **BIGGER**

kotecki

Following the RULES is an **EXCELLENT** way to fit in and avoid being questioned, laughed at, or scorned.

But it's not a particularly effective way of living an **AMAZING** story.

in fresno, california, no one may annoy a lizard in a city park.

In Elkhart, Indiana, it is illegal for barbers to threaten to cut off kids' ears.

In New York, women may go topless in public, providing it is not being used as a business.

Although impossible to track, there are probably hundreds of thousands of federal, state, and city laws in the United States, with new ones being proposed all the time. That doesn't count any of the rules enforced by schools and businesses.

Interestingly, with all of the laws and rules on the books, the ones we often cling to most fervently are the ones that don't actually exist.

you can't eat dessert first.

your socks must match.

adults should "act their age."

Most people have a hard time admitting that they're living by rules that don't exist. At first glance, it might be hard to even think of any. But if they were that easy to spot, you probably wouldn't be living by them in the first place. (Duh.) The trick is that they're sneaky and subconscious.

They're baked in, and reinforced by many years of repetition and adherence, so they seem normal to us. They are often disguised as conventional wisdom, which is dangerous, for as author Mark Stevens warns, "It is not wisdom. It is just convention. And convention often boils down to doing things the way they have always been done simply because they are done that way."

throughout our lives, starting at the very beginning, we are bombarded with these rules that don't exist.

This collection of "rules" come from a wide variety of sources: our best friends, first-grade teachers, parents, grandparents, politicians, old dead white guys, and even young celebrity trendsetters sporting more silicone than a nonstick bakeware factory. If we want to be successful, popular, get a good grade, or avoid death cramps when swimming, we listen to their advice.

We follow them (often subconsciously) for reasons that range from irrelevant to superstitious to downright stupid.

Some rules were established for practical reasons. And even though the reason for which they were created is no longer relevant, they live on. For instance, the reason our keyboard is laid out into a haphazard alphabet soup is not the effort of some drunk illiterate. Quite the contrary. In 1875, Christopher Sholes (his peeps called him Mr. Typewriter), ran into a problem with his new invention. The dang keys kept sticking together when a typist worked too quickly. Unable to figure out how to keep the keys from actually sticking, he decided the next best thing was to keep the typist from typing too fast. So he scientifically jumbled up the letters so that the commonest ones were spread apart. These days, jamming typewriter keys are only a problem for people who've been sleeping since 1984. But the QWERTY style keyboard layout is probably with us forever.

I grew interested in this topic when my wife, Kim, and I began our inaugural voyage through The Escape Plan and she nearly made a poor waitress's head explode. She obliterated the age-old "rule" that you're not supposed to eat dessert first by ordering chocolate lasagna as a first course at the Olive Garden. (More on that later.) Before long, I started to

notice all kinds of rules that don't exist, and I've been inspired by all sorts of people who make a point to break them regularly.

Now, there is something that quite likes the fact that we are easily prone to adhering to these rules that don't exist.

that something is Adultitis.

Adultitis is a sinister epidemic that transforms people into zombie-like doo-doo heads and makes the Black Death look like a trip to Disneyland.

the signs of Adultitis

officially, **ADULTITIS** is a common condition occurring in people between the ages of 21–121, marked by chronic dullness, mild depression, moderate to extremely high stress levels, a general fear of change, and, in some extreme cases, the inability to smile. Patients can appear aimless, discontent, and anxious about many things. Onset can be accelerated by an excess burden of bills, overwhelming responsibilities, or a boring work life. Generally, individuals in this condition are not fun to be around.

For more information about this terrible disease, including a test to see if you have it and ways to help stop its spread, please visit **http://adultitis.org.**

{ if you obey
all the rules
you miss all
the fun.

– katharine hepburn –

For a long time, Adultitis has gone unnoticed by the medical community, primarily because most of the officials who are in position to diagnose and treat patients often have Adultitis themselves, which at best clouds their judgment or in worst-case scenarios, causes them to deny Adultitis even exists.

But it does exist. And it has left in its wake a trail of broken, boring, and uninspired lives.

one of the most effective first steps in an attack on Adultitis is by identifying and breaking the rules that don't exist.

Because following these so-called rules is an amazingly terrific way to make sure your life sucks.

THIS is what a doughnut with chocolate frosting and sprinkles looks like when my daughter Lucy is done eating it.

I've never seen an adult eat a doughnut like this. Clearly, she doesn't know the proper way to eat a doughnut. Yet. One more thing we're gonna have to teach her, I thought as I snapped this photo.

Funny thing, though.

The doughnut police didn't break down the doors and take away her doughnut-eating license for "doing it wrong."

Sometimes I ask the audiences I speak in front of for examples of rules they live by that don't actually exist. I've never had anyone raise their hand and say, "You know, I don't know why I do it, but I always eat the whole doughnut even though sometimes I really just want to eat the frosting and sprinkles."

But those people exist. Maybe you're one of them.

Instead, I usually just get silence. People have trouble coming up with rules that don't exist. That's because we don't even know we're living by them; they're hardwired into the minutia of our everyday lives.

Even though this book only tackles forty of them, Lucy's doughnut makes me think that the actual number of these rules might be well into the millions.

I hope that this guide will serve as a reminder to be on guard against anyone who tells you that you can't eat dessert first, that your socks must match, or that there's a certain way to eat a doughnut.

I also hope it's a catalyst to break some rules in your own life, allowing you to create a better story for yourself and make Adultitis go running for the hills.

After all, there's no law on the books advising against that.

shine
on.

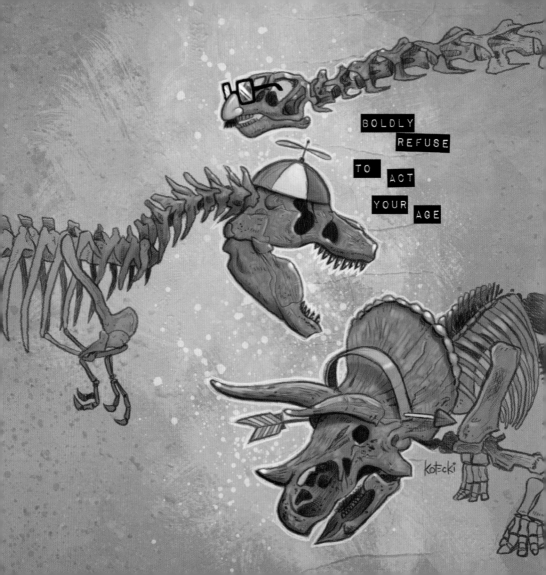

thou shalt act thine age

Of all the rules that don't exist, perhaps the most widespread is the notion that you are supposed to act your age.

I'm guessing that this quip originated from a woman who caught her husband throwing his shoe at the television while watching a football game. Or perhaps a high school teacher who was tired of his students firing spitballs across the classroom.

As with any rule, there usually contains within it a kernel of common sense. In this case, it is, "Quit acting like an idiot, you moron."

The problem with this rule is that it falls apart the minute you start to follow the logic. As the saying goes, "I do not know how to act my age. I have never been this age before." Furthermore, I have yet to find the handbook that details exactly how one is supposed to act upon reaching a certain age. For instance, which actions are supposed to be jettisoned when a thirty-seven-year-old turns thirty-eight? And when I turn sixty-five, am I suddenly supposed to jack my thermostat up to one hundred degrees, start eating dinner at 4:00 in the afternoon, and commence complaining about how the kids are wearing their pants these days?

Clearly, this rule has some real problems.

Even worse, this particular adage oversteps its bounds and enslaves many people in the chains of Adultitis. In an effort to "act our age," ANY actions and attitudes that could in any way be considered childish are tossed out like the proverbial baby and his proverbial bathwater. We laugh less, especially not at silly jokes. We're more stressed, because we focus our attention exclusively on "serious" matters. Instead of being optimistic, we become "realistic" (which really means pessimistic, although we'd never admit it).

What a shame.

Because some of the qualities we are so eager to abandon are the very things that can reward us with the kind of life we so desperately crave. One that is adventurous. Passionate. Meaningful. And fun.

It has been said that the average four-year-old laughs around four hundred times a day while grown-ups clock in at around fifteen. There is some debate over the source and accuracy of this statistic, but any fool could tell you that when it comes to the average daily laugh quotient, the chasm between kids and adults is astronomical.

Which age would YOU rather act?

Perhaps you might be thinking, "Well of course it was easier to laugh 400 times a day when I was four, Mister Smarty-Pants. I didn't have a job. I didn't have bills to pay. I didn't have kids!"

First of all, thank you for thinking me smart. But truly, I'd be a fool to argue with you. We do have more stresses and responsibilities than we did as children. So the bad news is that you are an adult. The good news is that you get to decide what that means.

The old flamethrower Satchel Paige has a question for you:

"how old would you be if you didn't know how old you are?"

If you feel unhappy, tired, stressed-out, bored, unadventurous, or any other negative emotion, try acting in the opposite way. To feel happier, act happier. To feel more adventurous, act more adventurously.

{ **boldly refuse to act your age.** }

– william james –

William James, philosopher and psychologist, declared, "Action seems to follow feeling, but really action and feeling go together; and by regulating the action, which is under more direct control of the will, we can indirectly regulate the feeling, which is not."

Indeed, acting yourself to a new way of thinking is easier than thinking your way to a new way of acting.

From now on, instead of acting your age, act more like the person you want to become.

thou shalt color inside the lines

Ever since you were able to hold a crayon, you've been instructed to color inside the lines.

If you consistently color inside the lines, you are heaped with praise and judged to be a budding artist with tremendous upswing. The kids who regularly color outside the lines? Well, we'd rather not talk about them.

Once you've mastered the art of coloring inside the lines, you need to make sure your color choices are proper as well. Blue for sky and green for trees, that sort of thing.

It's all a big smoke screen. None of this does anything to solidify your standing as a true artiste. (In fact, it encourages the opposite.) What it really does is teach you how to conform.

Conformity is the goal governments have for their citizens, factories have for their workers, and teachers have for their students. It gets you to follow the law, do the job, and fill in the little ovals on tests. All without asking too many questions (or ideally, none). Unfortunately, in our current world, governments have gotten too big for their own good, factories are closing down, and a diploma is less valuable than it's ever been.

The ability to color inside the lines may be a good test to see how well young children are developing their fine motor skills. The problem is that the continual reinforcement to color inside the lines when we were kids gets stuck in our psyche. Many of us carry it with us our entire lives.

It causes you to question whether or not you should take that risky dream job when you already have a secure job with good benefits. It makes you pause before putting action behind your most fantastic thoughts. It keeps you from deviating from the directions or straying too far from society's status quo.

Look at the cars we drive. In 1909, Henry Ford said, "Any customer can have a car painted any color that he wants so long as it is black." In 2009—exactly one hundred years later—the two most popular car colors were black and white. (And the next two most popular colors were gray and silver, which are a combination of the first two!) Add in blue and red, and those six colors make up 89 percent of all cars. "Other" clocks in at less than 1 percent.

I was speaking at a conference for early childhood educators and had the pleasure of hearing Lisa Murphy (aka The Ooey Gooey Lady) present. She told a story about doing a lesson on the letter "P" back when she was teaching.

She spread out a big white sheet and asked the kids to sit along the perimeter, a "p" word she explained to the kids, who had no idea what a perimeter was. Once all the kids were finally settled, she put an air pop popcorn machine in the middle of the sheet, poured in some kernels, and plugged it in. Without the top. Of course, as the popcorn popped, it flew everywhere, much to the delight and amazement of the children. One boy got a piece (aha! Another "p" word!) caught in his teeth, so Lisa taught him how to pick it out. (There's another "p" word!) The kids wanted to do it again, so she did, and the freshly popped corn was celebrated with much jubilation, as if they were seeing it for the first time. And the lesson turned into a party. (Yet another "p" word!)

At recess, all the children were buzzing to the other kids about what great fun they had with popcorn. About an hour later, a little girl, as if she was reminiscing over some long lost memory, said, "Miss Lisa, remember that one time we popped popcorn on that big sheet? Can we do it again?"

As Lisa told the story, she acknowledged that too many early childhood professionals would have said no, because it wasn't on the "schedule." They are too caught up in making sure that everything gets done. They are more focused on the to-do list than what might actually make for better learning.

On that day, however, in Lisa's classroom, popcorn popping took precedent.

It occurred to me that for many educators, slavishly following the schedule of preplanned curriculum is a rule that doesn't exist. It feels a lot like coloring outside the lines.

Then I realized that this rule is not exclusive to educators.

Following a schedule is a rule that most people follow, to the detriment of their own happiness. We can get more focused on the to-do list than we do on actually living.

You don't have to do the same thing you've always done, just because that's how (and when) you've always done them.

Eating dinner later because your family is in the middle of a heated board game is ok.

Letting go of your detailed vacation plan when you discover a hidden attraction that has rendered you spellbound is okay.

And taking the long way to your destination so you can fully enjoy a magnificent sunset is okay, too.

Conformity is a very good thing for governments, corporations, and schools. But not so much for you.

As adults, the only real reward for being the best at coloring inside the lines is a small measure of security. But it can come at the cost of unfulfilled potential and a boring story.

Jesus. Ghandi. Mother Teresa. Martin Luther King Jr. Amelia Earhart. Walt Disney. Harriet Tubman. John Lennon. Joan of Arc. George Washington. The greatest, most inspiring figures in the history of mankind have one thing in common: They were nonconformists.

they colored WAY outside the lines.

You were created to be something special, unlike anyone else who has or will ever live. You are called to stand out and shine like the stars.

Don't be afraid to ignore the instructions, ditch the schedule, or dance when others sit on the sidelines.

Don't be afraid to zig when others zag.

Don't be afraid to color outside the lines.

3

thou shalt not wear white after labor day

This one is a real doozy. Break this rule, and the fashion police will hunt you down and dress you in a baby blue butterfly-collared leisure suit with matching neckerchief.

The so-called "rule" that one should never wear white after Labor Day has been with us for many years. Interestingly, even fashion world experts can't agree on where this rule came from—and yet many people still abide by it. Ridiculous!

One educated guess is that during the summer, people wear white clothing because it helps keep them cooler. Naturally, you don't want to mess up your nice white stuff with mud and slush in the fall and winter. Hence the helpful— albeit somewhat obvious—guideline.

More likely is the idea that back in the day (meaning early twentieth century), most people that lived in cities wore dark-colored clothing. White linen suits and Panama hats became the unofficial look of the hoity-toities who escaped to the country for weekends of fun and leisure. Then older society families became concerned about the fashion etiquette of the "new rich," so they established a complex code of fashion rules to guide them. It was a way for the insiders to keep other people out, and a way for savvy outsiders to earn a ticket into polite society by proving they knew the rules.

Eventually, this no-white-after-Labor-Day statute leaked out and went mainstream in the 1950s and 1960s, and is still a big rule of thumb for many people today.

There is some debate as to the validity of this latter theory, but it makes the most sense to me. After all, pretty much every fashion rule is designed to label some as "in" and others as "out." (All the cool kids are wearing their jeans like this.)

Indeed, even Valerie Steele, director of the Museum at the Fashion Institute of Technology admits, "Very rarely is there actually a functional reason for a fashion rule."

Frankly, I don't think any of us should be listening to any fashion rules. It's a recipe for a future filled with some very awkward and embarrassing photos.

I don't care what decade you were in high school, no one would be caught dead in the stuff they were wearing in their yearbook photos. I think back to my middle and high school years, when girls flaunted foot-high walls of bangs cemented by six cans of Aqua Net hairspray. And the bottoms of our jeans were rolled so tightly that they threatened to cut off the circulation in our legs. (I had several friends lose feet in the early '90s.)

the '80s alone gave us shoulder pads, parachute pants, and neon. lots and lots of neon.

good call, fashion police.

Here's an iron-clad guarantee: The people who will look most ridiculous twenty years from now are pop stars and the people hosting shows like *What Not to Wear*.

It all comes down to our flawed propensity to care about what other people think. One of the coolest things about kids is they don't give a hoot what other people think. If a little girl wants to wear a tutu and cowboy boots with her favorite green sweater to church on a summer day, that's what she'll wear. (Unless Mom makes her change because she's worried about what other people think.)

If you want to break free from Adultitis, don't worry so much about trends and fashion rules with questionable origins.

Just be yourself and wear what you want.

because feeling comfortable in your own skin is one thing that never goes out of style.

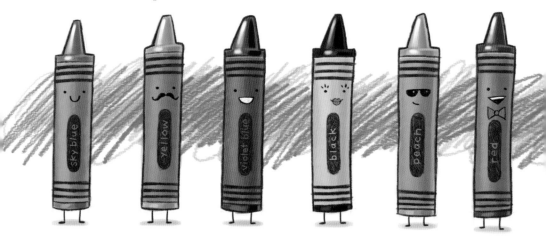

kotecki

29

thou shalt not celebrate without thine calendar's permission

Too many people treat the calendar as the utmost authority on what constitutes a good reason to celebrate. If a holiday is written in fine print on a particular day in the calendar, we assume it's safe to throw a party.

So, if the calendar says it's Halloween, we dress up in costumes and go bobbing for apples. If the calendar says it's Independence Day, then we'll throw meat on the grill and go blow something up. If the calendar says it's New Year's Eve, we stay up late, wear funny hats, and use instruments made of paper to make noises that sound like diptheria-ridden ducks.

Contrary to popular belief, your calendar is not the boss of you.

Making your last mortgage payment is a good reason to throw a party.

The night before the last day of school is a good reason to throw a party.

Baby's first laugh is a good reason to throw a party.

If a reason seems good enough to you, well then, it's good enough.

Heck, you can even create your own holiday if you want. If you'd like to be all official about it, you can register your holiday with *Chase's Calendar of Events*. But that's not a requirement.

A lady I met at a speaking engagement in Orlando told me about her son who lives in San Francisco. In honor of his birthday, he started putting homemade signs up everywhere that said, "June 1st is Pirate's Day." That's it. He put them on trains, telephone poles, and other public hot spots. And sure enough, June 1st came around and people could be spotted wearing eyepatches and various pirate gear.

Granted, San Francisco is known for being a little eccentric. But I'm willing to bet you could have similar results if you tried this in your workplace, your neighborhood, or even your own home.

> **turns out all you really need to start your own holiday is a little imagination, a few signs, and some courage.**

You know what else? You can even move a holiday to a completely different date if you really want to, like one family I know did.

I met Kevin and his family when I was in college. They were very involved in the church I attended. Such cool people: kind, warm, and welcoming. The parents modeled a marriage worth emulating. Kevin reminded me of me when I was his age: brown curly hair, thoughtful, and a little bit shy.

I'd lost touch, but got reconnected through the amazing power of Facebook. It saddened me to hear that Kevin, just twenty-three years old, was battling leukemia. He had been in Texas getting treatment and fighting hard, but with the cancer on the verge of winning the war, the doctors delivered the hard news that Kevin probably only had weeks to live.

This was especially discouraging because Kevin had hoped he'd be able to make it through one more Christmas, his favorite holiday. It was only

September. So with heavy hearts, the family returned home. But upon driving home from the airport, they noticed a curious thing as they turned into their subdivision.

The street was strewn with signs welcoming Kevin home. Beautiful red bows adorned their maple trees, fence, and porch. The neighbor's house bore Christmas lights, too. Inside their home, the stockings were hung, the halls were decked, and the aroma of cookies permeated the air. Friends and family gathered around the fully decorated Christmas tree to sing carols, led by Kevin and his dad on guitar.

Awesome.

Kevin made it to the "real" Christmas before passing away early in the new year. He and his family were a powerful and humbling example to me of what faith and love really look like during the difficult times. And as for the specific dates on which we're supposed to celebrate things like Halloween or Thanksgiving or Christmas?

They reminded me that those are optional, too.

the calendar as we know it is woefully incomplete. **every single day is a holiday.** it's just that most days, what to celebrate is up to you.

{ **rules are not necessarily sacred, principles are.** }

– franklin d. roosevelt –

LiFE iS SHORT

EAT DESSERT FiRST.

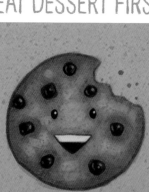

thou shalt not eat dessert first

Pretend that you are five. And it's dinnertime.

If I were to ask you, "Would you like to have dessert first tonight?", what would your reaction be? Kind of a no-brainer, right? You'd probably wonder if it was some sort of trick question because the answer would be so freaking obvious:

YES!

Kids are always looking to score a cookie before dinner or move on to cake before the carrots are consumed. But somewhere along the line, Mom, Dad, Grandma, or Grandpa says, "No, you can't have dessert first. It'll spoil your dinner."

Drat.

Disgruntled, you make a little promise to yourself that when you get big, you'll eat dessert whenever and wherever you want. When you get big, you'll live by your own rules. And yet . . . the majority of people probably can't remember the last time they had dessert first. Can you?

Kim and I went to the Olive Garden a few years ago, and in response to Escape Plan challenge #11, which implores you to do something your parents would never let you do as a kid, Kim ordered dessert first. The waitress had already written down my request for the manicotti with meat sauce, and began staring at Kim like she had lobsters coming out of her ears when she asked for the Chocolate Lasagna to arrive before her entrée.

The waitress was dumbstruck. Every time she returned to our table to refill our breadsticks, she commented on Kim's decision. "I just can't believe you're ordering dessert first," she began. "It's just that, well, nobody does that! I mean, sometimes people come in and just order dessert, but this, nobody does this! I've asked everybody in the back and they've never seen it, either. But you are . . . why?"

Kim simply said, "Because I can."

This is a perfect example of a rule we don't dare break, even though the consequences for doing so are zip. Zilch. Zero. Maybe we are afraid that the waitress will say no or think we're weird. Or that Mom will jump out from behind a fern and tell us to act our age, embarrassing us in front of everybody.

or perhaps we are so riddled with Adultitis that our inner child can't even be heard anymore.

We have been programmed with rules from a very early age, mostly by well-intentioned adults, but also by some nefarious ones as well. Some of the rules still serve us well (like "be kind to others"). But many of them are outdated or irrelevant (just a few of which I write about in this book). And most have gone unquestioned by Adultitis-ridden minds on autopilot.

Interestingly, my friend Jesse started a kick where he ordered dessert first, and actually developed some convincing arguments why it's a perfectly rational thing to do. For one, dessert at a restaurant is always ready. You can eat this immediately while they are cooking your other food, which is excellent when you're really hungry.

Secondly, this practice ensures you have room for dessert as you are eating it first. Then if you start getting full on your actual meal, just don't finish it and save it for later. However, if you fill up on your main meal first, you will likely either skip dessert, or order it anyway and overeat. This prevents overeating and ensures dessert consumption.

I like the way he thinks!

Now, am I saying that we should all eat dessert first for every meal? No, of course not. What I am saying is, why not do it once in a while? (You know you want to!)

The fact that we are so hesitant to even consider having our cake and eating it first points to an even bigger question:

what other rules are you unnecessarily living by?

kotecki

thou shalt not have too much fun at work

We are in a war against Adultitis. Especially at work.

Putting googly eyes on inanimate objects, decorating your cube for Halloween, and making cupcakes for coworkers are some of the weapons we have on our side.

Too bad some people prefer keeping them locked away.

I spoke at a conference for 911 operators recently. Afterward, a woman told me what a drag it is working at her dispatch center. "It didn't used to be that way," she said sadly. "We used to keep toys at our work stations and had a lot of fun decorating our offices for every holiday. But our new boss doesn't allow it. He thinks we should be more serious. It's really affected the morale of our whole team, and even officers who stop in ask where our decorations went."

Stories like this make me sad and angry all at once. Stories like this remind me why burnout is so rampant in today's workforce. It is possible to LOVE what you do but HATE where you work, and burnout happens when people work in such an environment.

Burnout can be easily resolved. But it requires leaders who see the power in bringing fun in to the workplace and are smart enough to understand that having a little fun in no way diminishes the seriousness in which one takes his or her responsibility.

I can't imagine many more serious occupations than being a 911 dispatcher. On a regular basis, they hear screams of terror and horrible tales of human suffering. And with great professionalism and compassion, they listen and they offer help. To think that anyone can survive—let alone thrive—in an environment like this without a little fun and humor is just plain idiotic.

I'll admit, sometimes I feel inadequate for suggesting some of the ideas that I do in my talks. They are as silly as they are simple. I imagine the people with crossed arms wondering, "Who actually paid this guy real money to tell us THIS?"

Too many leaders see something like decorating an office as a frivolous waste of time. Even if they acknowledge a morale problem, they refuse to believe that such simple solutions can be effective. And that's where they're wrong. We human beings worship complexity, but the truth is that the simplest solutions are often the ones that work best.

simplicity is the ultimate sophistication.

Our world is aching for silliness. Not just in the backyard, but in the board-room as well.

Examples of smart companies that use whimsy to attract top talent, foster collaboration, and prevent burnout abound. Google offices are famous for featuring things like fireman's poles and slides. Epic Systems Corporation, a company located in Verona, Wisconsin, makes software for medical groups, hospitals, and integrated health-care organizations, has a conference room that looks like a treehouse and an office hallway modeled after the New York subway. And UK juice-maker Innocent installed a Twister game in their elevator.

We hear it time and time again: People like doing business with people they like. Well, aren't people who are having a blast at what they're doing more fun than people who aren't?

The greatest news is that it's pretty easy (and profitable) to add a little childlike spirit to any workplace. Let's use a receptionist as an example, because so many businesses have one in some form. Too many of them are reminiscent of Roz from *Monsters, Inc.*, grumpily barking warm greetings like, "Name and ID, please."

Marketing guru Seth Godin wrote a post on his blog entitled, "How to be a great receptionist." He offered a number of easy ideas that a good receptionist could use to transform herself (or himself) into a GREAT receptionist. Many had a childlike spin to them. Here are a few:

- **I'd argue for a small budget to be spent on a bowl of M&M's or the occasional Heath Bar for a grumpy visitor.**

- **If you wanted to be really amazing, how about baking a batch of cookies every few days?**

- **I'd ask the entire organization for updates as to who is coming in each day: "Welcome Ms. Mitchell. How was your flight in from Tucson?" (A nice way to interject a little curiosity.)**

- **Is there a TV in reception? Why not hook up some old Three Stooges DVDs?**

Candy? Cookies? The Three Stooges? What is this, an out-of-control Kindergarten classroom? Nope. It's an office that understands that the receptionist is just as important a part of the company's brand as that high-priced TV ad, fancy business card, or freshly painted fleet of company cars. (Probably more so, actually.)

As Seth points out, "Think the job-acceptance rate goes up if the first impression is a memorable one? Think the tax auditor might be a little more friendly if her greeting was cheerful?"

Decorating the office, empowering your receptionist to be more childlike, and adding a little whimsy to your products or packaging may be simple, but they actually do something quite important.

they have the power to uplift the human spirit.

When we as humans tap into that power, adding a sense of playfulness and whimsy to the world around us, magic happens. We connect with something supernatural. Something good. Something that elevates the human condition.

P. T. Barnum once said, "The noblest art is that of making others happy." Whether you are a business owner or an artist or a marketer or a school teacher or an architect—whatever you are—never underestimate the power of a smile. Whenever you can bring a little gladness and gaiety to someone's day, do it. Ignore the naysayers with Adultitis; there is nothing superfluous or trivial about it. It's one of the reason's you're here.

having fun at work is simple. profitable. and gravely important.

Conversations like the one I had with that 911 dispatcher leave me ever more convinced that if we really want to win this serious war against Adultitis, we need to get serious about having fun.

Especially at work.

thou shalt not jump in puddles

Several years ago, Kim and I were hanging out at the Memorial Union on the University of Wisconsin campus in Madison. Overlooking Lake Mendota, it's the perfect place to sit in one of the trademark yellow, orange, or green chairs and people watch.

On this day, my eyes were drawn to a small family—Mom, Dad, and a little girl with pigtails—walking along the shoreline. The girl was a few yards ahead of her parents when she spotted a puddle, a remnant of the rainstorm that had drenched the city the day before.

Like the Millennium Falcon being pulled toward the Death Star by its powerful tractor beam, the girl was drawn to the pool of water.

Her intent was clear: She was going to get up close and personal with that puddle.

My first reaction was strong and immediate: "Nooooo!"

I don't remember how the parents reacted, but I was shocked at what my reaction said about me: I was officially a grown-up. The little girl's primal urge was to pounce through that puddle, while mine was to pull her away. No greater chasm exists than the space between those two extremes. There was a time when I was on her team, but at some point when I wasn't paying attention, I inadvertently switched sides.

Hoodwinked by Adultitis.

Most people do switch sides at some point in their life. I suspect it happens at different times for different people. Perhaps the moment is directly cor-related to the time at which one becomes responsible for doing their own laundry. Or maybe a soul can only take so many stern rebukes and warnings to stay out of the rain and puddles.

I find it humorous that we grown-ups eagerly drench ourselves in long showers, immerse ourselves in tubs infused with bath oils with names like Lavender Rain, and spend hundreds of dollars to get soaked at super-size water parks, and yet we treat a simple puddle like a pool of hydrochloric acid and we run from the rain like the Wicked Witch of the West running for her life.

Like all rules that don't exist, this one is propped up by some pretty confusing logic. Apparently a grown man can scream like a schoolgirl while hurtling down a high water slide, but should he dance through a puddle like Gene Kelly, he gets labeled as crazy.

What's crazy is how we act when it does rain. We scurry from the store to our car like cockroaches who've just had the lights turned on. If we are without an umbrella, we desperately cover our heads with newspapers or flimsy pieces of plastic. We temporarily forget that wet clothes dry and mud washes out.

The fact is this: When you are an adult, there is nothing that makes you feel more foolish than getting soaked in the rain for no reason when a perfectly good shelter is only a few feet away.

But to a child, no sight is more foolish than a group of adults huddling under shelter when there is perfectly good rain to dance in only a few feet away.

Two sides. Two choices. Only one makes you feel more alive. The cool thing about being an adult is that you get to pick.

It makes one wonder, are we truly living or are we just trying not to get our shoes wet?

thou shalt not eat breakfast for dinner

Some people just love eating breakfast for dinner. They talk about it giddily, as if they gave their boss a wedgie and got away with it.

Of course, when I speak of eating breakfast for dinner, I'm talking about those certain foods that, in certain cultures, have been exclusively relegated to certain mealtimes.

Eggs. Pancakes. Waffles. Orange juice. Froot Loops.

Eat them at other times of day and you're either a college student, a truck driver, or weird.

Now perhaps this rule was brought about by a clever and successful marketing conspiracy by the titans of Eggs, Pancakes, and their friends. By being tied to a specific meal, they could DOMINATE that meal. And dominate they have. If that was indeed the case, then my hat is off to the titans of Eggs, Pancakes and friends. Well played. Grand slam.

But I'm pretty sure it's still legal to eat these foods for lunch or dinner as well, if you're so inclined.

And while we're on the subject, it's also okay to consume pizza, cake, or wine for breakfast.

Having breakfast for dinner isn't completely unheard of, but it is pretty rare. It's also a simple first step to break out of the rut Adultitis may have you in.

And if you really want to get Adultitis's panties in a bunch, go ahead and do it in your pajamas.

{ know the rules
well, so you can
break them
effectively.

– dalai lama xiv –
}

thou shalt hate monday

Monday wishes he was Friday, or even Thursday. He has giant posters of Saturday on his bedroom wall. Everybody turns the other way when they see Monday walking down the hall.

Poor Monday.

I used to suffer from a condition known as Sunday Night Dread, that sinking feeling you get when the freedom of the weekend is gasping its last breath. I used to think Monday was the worst.

And then I realized that Monday is just a patsy.

It's convenient to throw Monday under the bus when we're unhappy about how our story is going. I propose that we quit picking on Monday and try a different tack. Here are a few options.

1) Change your attitude. The easy and smart choice is to find more meaning in the work you already do. There is no perfect job. Even though I don't dread Mondays anymore, not every part of my job is peachy keen. But I focus on the good stuff, which far outweighs the bad stuff. If you are honestly in a job that is a good fit for you and that you actually enjoy—but still dislike Mondays—perhaps you can try on a new perspective. List out all of the things you love about your job and focus on those instead of the negatives. Or, if you're simply bored with your current job, maybe it's time to initiate a new project that excites you. It will give you a new spark and sense of purpose (and will probably impress your boss).

2) Change your job. An equally smart choice, but a little harder, is to start taking action toward finding some new work with more meaning. Life is too short to be stuck in a job you hate, or even one you only kind of like. Find one that makes you excited to get up in the morning, eager to share your gifts and tackle the challenges in front of you. Of course, this is not something you can magically wave a magic wand to achieve. It's not recommended to up and quit a crappy job without a plan, for in almost all cases, a crappy job is better than no job. What you CAN do is make a plan. Figure out what might be a better fit, and start taking baby steps to get there. It might involve taking some night classes. Or getting up an hour early to send out resumes. Or building that web site for your new part-time business. The Mondays in your immediate future may not be too appealing, but at least you'll know you're not resigned to a lifetime of them.

Warning! Some people may be tempted to ease up on Monday in order to cast dispersions on what they perceive as the bigger problem, which is work in general.

Many people dream about winning the lottery so they can quit their soul-sucking job and go spend their days lying on a beach, sipping margaritas, and soaking up rays, thereby putting Monday in the cool group with all the other days.

Only one problem.

Such an existence would get boring, and fast.

Oh sure, it would be heaven at first. I have no beefs against vacations. But we're not talking about vacation here, remember? This is your new life. And after two or three weeks (maybe after three months, depending on how much soul-sucking your job did), you would start to get restless. You'd start craving something meaningful to do.

We often get duped into believing that work is the villain holding us back from

Key Lime State of mind

the perfect life. If only we could figure out how to work less—or better yet, not at all!—then we'd really be happy. But work, like Monday, is just another patsy.

The REAL key to happiness (and so-called work-life balance) is not figuring out how to work less, but doing more work that matters.

They say that if you love your work, it never feels like work. I'm not sure about that. I love my work, but there are parts of it that still feel an awful lot like work. That said, the fact that I love what I do makes the work—even the hard parts—worthwhile.

The hallmark of way too many "adult" lives is the propensity to "live for the weekends." The workweek is meant to be muddled through, a necessary evil required to pay the bills and finance the epic fun we are finally allowed to have on the weekend. But the drama they indulge in is only a temporary fix that always ends with the cold shower known as Monday morning.

Instead of escaping by means of cheap thrills, strong drinks, or mindless entertainment, might I suggest a more productive, long-term fix?

Escape instead from the rules that don't exist but that are currently holding you back. Practice being courageous and begin to dream again. Let go of the assumptions that the workweek must always be drudgery and that passionate living can't be a daily reality. Ask questions about your current situation and get curious about what some new choices might manifest. Tap into your wellspring of passion and work at becoming the linchpin you were created to be.

if friday is your favorite day of the week, it might be time to make a change.

Getting your story to the point where Mondays don't suck is not easy. But it is doable. It just takes a bit of honesty, a plan, some hard work, and maybe a new attitude, all of which are things you can do, starting today.

After all, poor Monday has been bullied enough, don't you think?

freedom

thou shalt brag about how busy thou art

When did busyness become a badge of honor, a way to brag about how successful we are?

Ask anyone how they're doing and the answer is "Great! Keeping busy!" "So busy!" "Crazy busy!"

It is a boast disguised as a complaint.

Apparently, whoever is the busiest wins. (Although I'm not sure what.) Just once, it would be cool to hear someone say, "I haven't been very busy at all. I'm just taking life as it comes, enjoying it one moment at a time."

After observing people in restaurants, airports, and elsewhere, I actually think many people crave busyness. It's as if they self-induce busyness in order to feel better about themselves. More valued. More important.

Maybe constantly being on the phone in public makes them feel like a big shot.

Maybe busyness numbs them from some pain they don't want to deal with.

Maybe busyness serves as a convenient distraction to avoid or postpone hard and scary changes they need to make.

Taking the drug called busyness is an effective way to feel engaged in life. But although it's easier to stay busy than to slow down and make hard decisions about what kind of story you really want to live, the end result is not very satisfying.

warning: if you measure your level of importance and value by how busy you are, there's a pretty good chance the story you're living sucks.

If you've chosen busyness as a lifestyle choice—yes, Virginia, it's a choice— more power to you.

Somewhere, Adultitis is smiling widely.

thy christmas cookies shalt look like christmas cookies

Even if you don't celebrate Christmas, I'm sure you can conjure up an image of what Christmas cookies are "supposed" to look like. And although there are many different kinds of Christmas cookies, I'm guessing this is not the image that comes to mind first.

Believe it or not, these are, in fact, Christmas cookies. And they were not made by a four-year-old or a victim of the Great Kitchen Catastrophe of '73.

The story of these so-called Ugly Cookies goes like this:

One year, Terry was overwhelmed with all the things she had to do to get ready for a Christmas party. With a list a mile long and not much time to complete it, she decided that she'd try a newfangled thing called delegation.

So she turned to her husband and son.

"I have to run some errands before the guests arrive tonight. You guys are in charge of the Christmas cookies," she ordered. "Here's the recipe. There are only a few steps and a handful of ingredients. Just do exactly what it says."

Since the husband and son loved Christmas cookies—especially the eating part—this was a good thing. But as they gathered the supplies, conversation shifted to how unfair it was that every year, Mom made these cookies for guests and they never got to eat any of them. And so they concocted a diabolical scheme.

rather than making more cookies, they decided to make them as disgusting looking as possible so no one else would want to eat them.

Black, brown and army green frosting took center stage. Normal Christmas cookie cutters were abandoned for shapes like cows, race cars, and hands. Not mittens, hands.

When Mom returned home and saw the finished batch of ugly cookies, she was horrified. But it was too late to make new ones. So she positioned herself at the front door as guests arrived, and made sure that she told every visitor, "I did NOT make the cookies!" When people heard the story, they

laughed. And when they saw them, they laughed harder.

Eventually, one brave soul decided to try one (perhaps she had too much egg nog?), and discovered that they were, in fact, delicious. So the original plan of the husband and son failed. But they were not deterred. They resolved to try harder next year.

Eventually, they branched out into cakes.

The guys broke the rule of what Christmas cookies (or a graduation cake, for that matter) is supposed to look like. And they created a tradition that has lasted for twenty years. Their goal, year after year, is to make the ugliest Christmas cookies around.

By the way, the mom is a big supporter of the tradition now. People look forward to it. In fact, her mother—the grandma—eventually requested an ugly birthday cake of her own.

What sorts of things do you do the exact same way every Christmas because you've ALWAYS done them that way?

What if you changed things up this year?

I'm not talking about the sacred, untouchable family traditions (although maybe I am). But what about the things you do automatically, without much thought and without any real meaning? After all, forgoing the stress that can come from trying to create a confection that might make Martha Stewart weep tears of joy is not nearly as fun as concocting something that would have her wailing and gnashing her teeth.

To take it a step further, what other things do you do every year, every month, every week, every day—at work or at home—because you've always done them that way? What opportunities could you uncover, what problems might you solve, what new memories might you create if you took a different tack?

going ugly can
have some
beautiful results.

thou shalt not blow bubbles in thy milk

Kim and I had a big test early on in our parenting adventure.

At dinner one evening when she was about two, Lucy got to drink out of a "big-girl cup" with a straw. And for the first time ever, she discovered how to blow bubbles in her milk. In our household, this is on par with first words, first steps, and learning how to dunk cookies in milk.

It's kind of a big deal.

The coolest part is that she figured it out on her own; we didn't have to teach her. It was awesome witnessing the moment of discovery, when surprise transformed into delight. However, when her cup had become entirely consumed by bubbles, she actually grew concerned and seemed disappointed when she asked, "Where did milk go?"

"Don't worry, it'll come back," I assured her.

And as the bubbles dispersed, it did! (One of the perks of parenting is presenting the illusion of being all-knowing.)

Naturally, blowing bubbles in her milk became much more interesting to Lucy than actually eating dinner. And Adultitis strongly encouraged both Kim and me to tell her to cut it out. The inner debate about how to proceed was more crucial than one might expect. For you see, we give out little cards to every person who attends one of our speaking programs, and it features this comic strip:

We've handed out thousands and thousands and thousands of these cards. Would we now become the parents who admonish our child for blowing bubbles in her milk? Kim and I exchanged a look that indicated we didn't want to be.

I stopped the inner conversation in my head and quickly analyzed the situation: What's the big deal? What are my main concerns? For one, I wanted to make sure she actually ate her dinner in a reasonable amount of time. And secondly, I was not especially keen on cleaning up any milk-bubble overflows.

So we made it clear that she needed to keep the straw (and the bubbles) in the glass. And after a few more minutes of bubble-blowing fun, we pulled the glass away and told her she could resume after she ate a few more bites of her dinner. I was amazed at the responsiveness we got! Inadvertently, we had turned blowing bubbles in milk into an incentive more powerful than M&M's (which up to that point, had been the currency of choice in our household)!

It's easy to jump into automatic mode in our roles as parents, teachers, or leaders and respond to situations in the same way we've seen other parents, teachers, and leaders do it, without ever stopping for just a second to question if there might be another way. Stopping that knee-jerk reaction is the hard part, but once we do, the other (better) way is not that hard to find.

That's why thinking about these rules that don't exist is such an important pastime. The more we do it, the more of them we recognize. And the easier it is to stop and search for a better way.

In the end, I think we passed the test by honoring one of the special joys of childhood while avoiding a mess and steering clear of turning into total pushovers. (It was nice to have some confidence going into potty training.)

Meanwhile, although it may not be a preferred habit for dinner parties and state dinners, my little personal wish for Lucy is that she never stops blowing bubbles in her milk.

{ rules are made
for people who
aren't willing
to make up
their own. }

– chuck yeager –

HOW DO YOU LOOK IN
YOUR BATHING SUIT
?
No Skinny
Scare-Crows
LIKE THIS?!
OR THIS
Try them without risking a cent
Special offer!
kotecki

thou shalt wait thirty minutes to swim after eating

No doubt you've heard the cautionary tale.

If you jump into a lake or swimming pool immediately after eating, there is a very high probability that you will cramp up and drown or get sucked into the pool filter or get eaten by lake sharks. Or something equally terrible.

False.

In his book, *25 Ways to Cure the Hiccups*, Dr. Brian Udermann of the University of Wisconsin–LaCrosse sets the record straight. There is not "one report of a drowning or near drowning due to swimming immediately after eating."

Here's the truth: When you eat, an increased supply of blood flows to your stomach and intestines to absorb the nutrients, meaning that there is less blood available to deliver oxygen and remove waste from exercising muscles. However, you have more than enough oxygen to do both activities just fine. In fact, according to Udermann, "an article on the topic published in 1961 by Arthur Steinhaus claims that the body will supply the exercising muscles with the blood and oxygen needed before diverting blood to the stomach.

"It has been suggested that the myth may have been perpetuated by older versions of the Red Cross First Aid Instructors book, which contained recommendations about not swimming after eating, and by such folklore as American Indians massaging the abdomen after meals to make swimming safe."

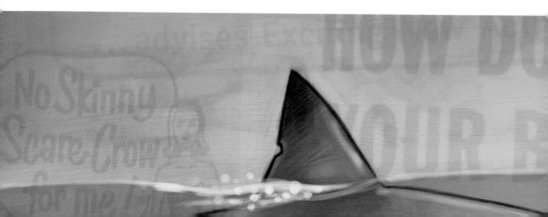

Most rules that don't exist are with us because they've picked up steam from one generation to the next. Your mom says it because she heard her mom say it. It's printed on the metal sign at the public pool so it must be serious.

The bad news is, we often follow rules that don't exist just because we've always followed them. Instead of following blindly, make a point to stop and ask why. A simple search on the Internet solved the case for me in five minutes.

The good news is that if you jump into the lake right after lunch, you're not gonna drown.

or get eaten by lake sharks.

thou shalt let others
define thy success

An exciting, important (and sometimes scary) by-product of looking at your life as a story is realizing that you are the head writer. It's actually one of the best parts about being a grown-up. No longer are you beholden to doing what your parents and teachers want you to do.

What a shame it is, then, that so many people coast through life accepting the plot other people have set out for them. After years spent being conditioned to follow instructions, we feel lost when there's no one telling us what to do. It's easy to fill the void with the opinions of others.

When I was doing research for this book, I asked a bunch of people to share their "favorite" rules that don't exist. Pamela Slim, author of *Escape from Cubicle Nation* and all-around awesome person, told me, "The one I believe all people should banish is, 'Thou shalt base your success on the opinions of your neighbors.' So often, we long for the success of others without considering what is truly important to us. Coveting the success of others is a true and direct path toward misery. Learn about yourself. Find what makes you truly happy. Write your own definition of success based on what makes you happy. Own it."

Amen, sister.

It's really easy to get swept into other people's version of success, causing you to lose track of your own. Some people want to change the world. Others want money. Or respect. Or fame. Or the freedom to do what they love.

I quite like Chris Garrett's definition: "Success is about living the life you want to live, waking up happy, and being with the people you want to share that life with."

This one's good, too: "Getting to do what you love to do everyday—that's really the ultimate luxury."—Warren Buffett

So here's a pop quiz: What is the opposite of success?

I'm no psychic, but I'm gonna go ahead and guess that you'd probably say that the opposite of success is failure.

That would be wrong. Professional speaker Joe Malarkey accurately points out that the opposite of success is actually doing nothing. In fact, failure is an integral part of success. Joe points out that all successful people have failed, they just didn't stay there very long.

Sometimes we see following the template of someone else's success as a surefire prescription for avoiding failure. We hate failing. We really hate losing. Most of us go to great lengths to avoid experiencing either.

Everyone who's ever learned to ride a bike failed. At least a few times. Sometimes so much so that you may have felt like filing a restraining order against the sidewalk. But time and time again, you got back up, slapped a Hello Kitty Band-Aid on your knee (just me?), and got back on your bike. With a little coaching, and a little persistence, you found it: success.

Failing isn't fun. But it's awfully hard to learn how to ride a bike sitting on your couch.

Remember, you are the head writer in the story starring you. Don't let other people dictate the direction of your blockbuster, and for the love of God, don't just sit there doing nothing.

Decide what your definition of success is and then go do that.

ACTION!

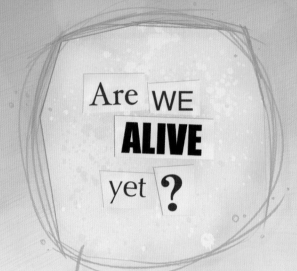

thou shalt do and see everything whilst on vacation

What do most people say when they return from vacation?

I need another vacation!

Why? Because they spent the whole time killing themselves trying to do and see everything. On the surface, it makes perfect sense. Oftentimes, vacations are a significant financial investment. And it may be the first and only time we get to experience the locations we visit. Certainly we should try and squeeze in as much as possible, right?

Thomas Merton suggests another way of looking at it in his book, *No Man Is an Island*. He writes:

"We do not live more fully merely by doing more, seeing more, tasting more, and experiencing more than we ever have before. On the contrary, some of us need to discover that we will not begin to live more fully until we have the courage to do and see and taste and experience much less than usual.

A tourist may go through a museum with a travel guide, looking conscientiously at everything important, and come out less alive than when he went in. He has looked at everything and seen nothing. He has done a great deal and it has only made him tired. If he stopped for a moment to look at one picture he really liked and forgotten about all the others, he might console himself with the thought that he had not completely wasted his time. He would have discovered something not only outside himself but in himself."

merton offers advice that slaps conventional wisdom in the face with a codfish. live more fully by experiencing less?

He's right, though, isn't he? Too often, our vacations do leave us more tired than when we departed, and we pine for another just to recover. Like Merton's museum visitor, we are convinced that we must do and see and taste everything (or at least as many of the things highlighted on that one travel show we saw).

How much richer would a visit to New York City be if instead of running around trying to see every single famous landmark, you spent an entire day immersed in the Ellis Island experience, or putzing around lazily in Central Park?

I am reminded of a vacation my family took to Door County, Wisconsin, a number of years ago. It was the first family vacation we'd been on since my brothers and I had grown up (I use that term loosely). During the day, we all went our separate ways. Kim and I went for a hike while my parents explored the local shops and my brother took his family on a bike ride. But at night, we'd reconvene to have dinner and spend time together around a campfire on the shores of Green Bay.

One particular evening, my niece produced a box of jelly beans. Mind you, these were not your normal every day jelly beans. They were the Harry Potter-themed Bertie Botts beans from Jelly Belly that featured flavors such as juicy pear and buttered popcorn intermingled with others like Vomit, Moldy Cheese, and Earthworm.

With the full moon and flickering flames providing our only light, someone got the bright idea of playing a game of Jelly Bean Russian Roulette. The concept was simple: pass the box around the fire, take a jelly bean, eat it, and try and guess the flavor.

My mom was not a fan of this idea. But to her credit, she played along. (It was my dad, however, who drew the proverbial short straw, with the seemingly never-ending rotation of sardine and vomit flavored jelly beans.)

We had a blast. So much so that we depleted the beans and had to buy a new box for the next night.

For those unaware, Door County is one of those typical vacation destinations with no shortage of things to do. Wine tastings. Fishing opportunities. Gallery visits. We did a lot of those things, but to a person, everyone's favorite memory of that time together were the starry nights around the campfire, laughing, sharing stories, and eating disgusting jelly beans.

It was unforgettable, and 100 percent unplanned. I am confident that we would have missed out on those memories had we not taken the time to just "be."

This idea of simplifying our life by doing less may be the message that this current generation needs to hear more than anything. It is the key to finding peace and happiness and the hidden ingredient of amazing, rejuvenating, life-giving vacations.

Instead of jamming as much activity into our leisure time as possible, let's give ourselves the gift of breathing room. Instead of spending our time watching the penguins at the zoo thinking about what four exhibits we should go see next, maybe we should just spend time, you know, actually watching the penguins.

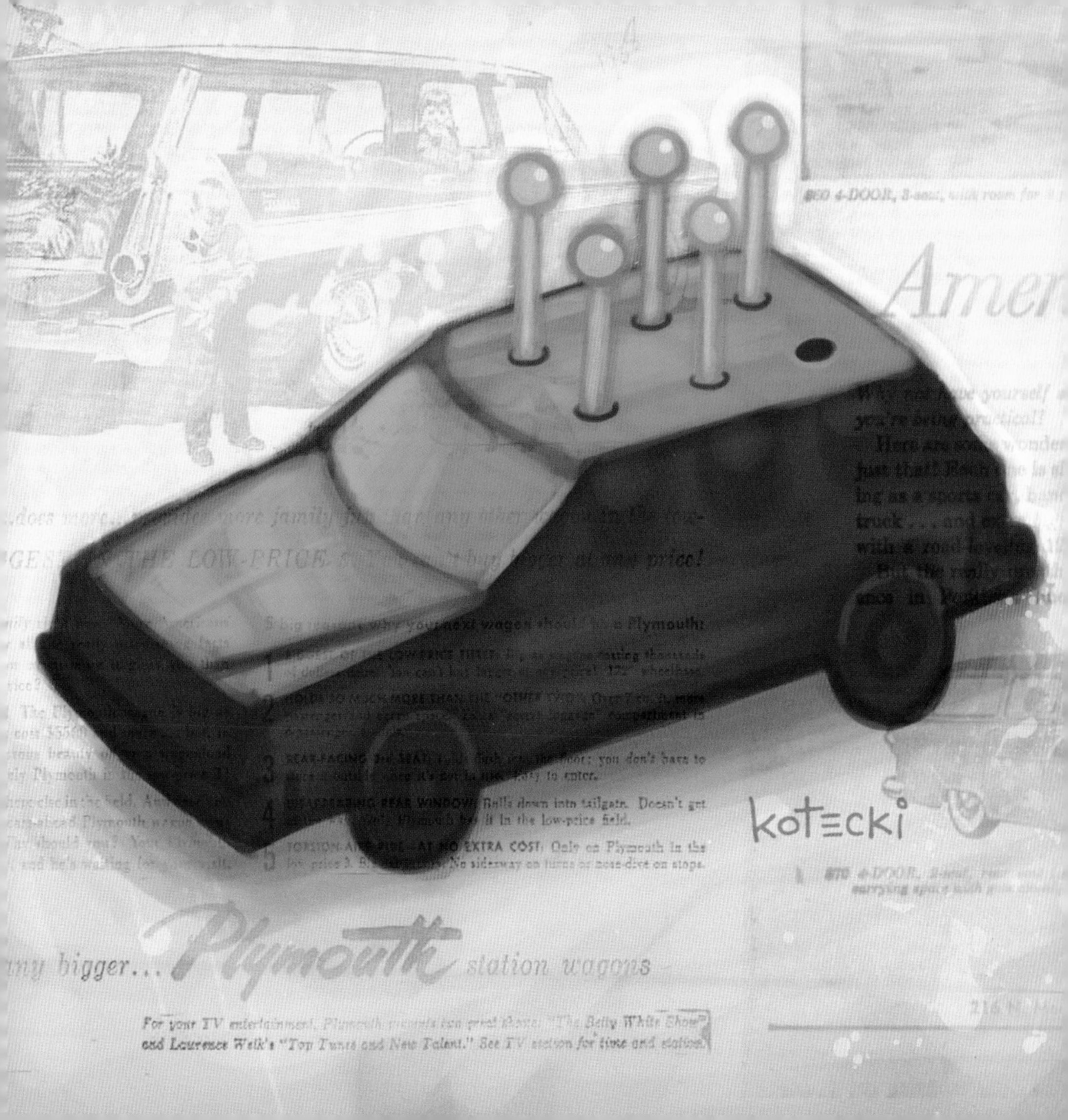

kotecki
ny bigger... Plymouth station wagons
Amer

life. | balance.

thou shalt clean thy plate

"Eat your beans! Don't you know that there are kids starving in Africa?"

Thanks to this little mantra, I always feel like I'm committing some grave sin anytime I leave food on my plate. It reminds me of the line in *It's a Wonderful Life*, when the little kid says, "Every time a bell rings, an angel gets its wings!" Except that in my case, for every forkful of food that remains on my plate, a child in Ethiopia dies.

I mean, I didn't grab those green beans from a girl in Ghana like a bully taking Tater Tots from a classmate. And if I could somehow teleport my leftovers to a hungry kid in Haiti right at that moment, I certainly would. Happily.

I'm not saying the world doesn't have a food-distribution problem. I'm just saying finishing everything on my plate isn't going to solve it.

On the other hand, sometimes I feel like leaving food behind is a waste of money. Just this morning, I was at a coffee shop writing this book. I bought a cinnamon roll that was as big as my head. Now, I didn't need a cinnamon roll as big as my head, but that's all they had. I felt full long before the cinnamon roll was finished but it killed me to throw the last of it away. It seemed like the equivalent of burning my wallet. But what's the alternative? I doubt the barista would oblige a request to pay half for a cinnamon roll as big as, say, a baby's fist.

when it comes to dishing out guilt and defending the rules that don't exist, Adultitis doesn't deal in logic.

It's been well documented that America has an obesity problem. Everybody has an opinion on how to solve it.

My friend Jill Fleming is a dietician who wrote a book called *Thin People Don't Clean Their Plate*.

I'm no medical expert, but that appears to be a pretty good place to start.

Give your waistline a gift and throw your guilt down the garbage disposal. You really don't have to clean thy plate.

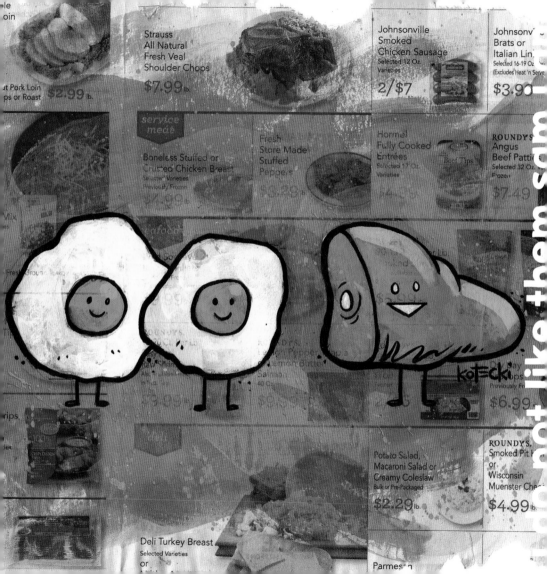

SUPER IS as SUPER does

thou shalt always wear clean underpants upon leaving thy house

Moms everywhere seem to be united in their desire to make sure that if we leave the house, we do so with clean underpants.

In case we get into an accident. Naturally.

Because if you get into an accident, and you are rushed to the hospital, and the emergency workers are required to remove your underwear, and they discover that your tighty-whiteys are not as white as they should be, your mother will be notified immediately about her automatic induction into the Bad Mom Hall of Shame.

Or so I gather.

"Did you hear Linda's boy was in an accident?"

"Yes, it's all over the news. I guess he's okay, but I heard from somebody who knows somebody that his underwear wasn't clean."

"What a shame. You know, I always had my doubts about that family."

Once I was in Grand Junction, Colorado, to speak at a conference for early childhood professionals. I got into a discussion with a lady from Denver who told me of a memorable drive through the mountains a year earlier. She was driving along, and out of nowhere, a massive boulder tumbled down the mountain and crashed right in front of her car. It was so enormous, she could feel the ground shake upon impact. Yikes. Fortunately, it didn't land on her car, and no one was injured.

So why interrupt the discussion about this important "rule" involving underwear with a tale of a giant rock?

Simple. If I'm driving down the road, minding my own business, and a multiton boulder lands a few feet from my vehicle, if I had clean underwear BEFORE the incident, I sincerely doubt they'd remain as such AFTER the incident.

In fact, if I was involved in ANY serious accident that required an emergency trip to a hospital in which people other than me were removing my underwear, I think it's safe to say that they'd be in a similar state of squalor.

Which leads me to conclude that wearing clean underpants, although the preferred way to go, is not as crucial as our mothers would have us believe.

perhaps the better rule to follow would be to watch for falling rocks.

Hello
my name is

BOB

kotecki

18

thou shalt remove thy nametag immediately after an event

You've been there. You've attended a conference, a retreat, a networking meeting, or some other event that required you to wear a nametag. And then, hours after the event is over, you look down in horror to find that you are STILL wearing it. It clings to your shirt, mocking you like a group of middle schoolers laughing at your generic bargain-buy shoes from Kmart.

Doh!

You shamefully reflect back to calculate how many people must have seen you wearing your idiocy on your shirt, but count yourself fortunate that you didn't have to undergo death by embarrassment from someone actually pointing out the faux pas to your face.

Because as everyone knows, although nametags are useful for things like networking meetings, they are to be removed IMMEDIATELY after such events.

Or are they?

Most of the hidden rules we live by don't seem all that much like rules. That's why we barely notice them. Removing your nametag immediately after an event doesn't seem so much like a rule as it does a good bit of common sense. Especially if you want to avoid giving off the impression that you're an absent-minded doofus.

Besides, who would even want to break a rule like that? There's too much to risk and nothing to gain.

Wanna bet?

My good friend Scott Ginsberg made a career out of wearing a nametag every day. After attending an event in college, he made the fateful decision to keep his nametag on instead of throwing it in the trash like everyone else did as they walked out the door. He's been wearing one every day since. For over thirteen years. Just over five thousand days straight as of this writing. He made a living writing, speaking, and consulting on becoming more approachable, his expertise drawn from all of the things he's learned through this experience. He's written a dozen books, he's been invited to a number of countries to speak, and he's been featured in media outlets such as *USA Today, 20/20*, and *The Wall Street Journal*.

All because he dared to break a rule that everyone else is afraid to break.

There is a lot to gain by breaking the rules you might not consider worth breaking.

living by them mindlessly?

now that's risky.

you are beautifull

kotecki

thou shalt conceal thy wrinkles

This one's for the ladies.

Full disclosure: At last check, I am not a woman. So I cannot claim to be an expert in the things women go through. But one thing I am sympathetic to is all of the messages bombarding you about your appearance. I mean guys have the pressure to maintain six-pack abs (I'm one sixth of the way there!), but it's nothing compared to the onslaught you face on a daily basis.

Let's take wrinkles, which are supposedly The Devil.

Apparently they are something to be avoided at all costs.

My wife has told me horror stories of going to parties at friends' homes in which she was fearfully warned about such evils as forehead rows, crow's feet, and turkey necks. Honestly, I'm not sure how they get away with calling these get-togethers "parties." Naturally, some sort of high-priced miracle balm is revealed that claims to have the power to prevent wrinkles, slow down the aging process, and stop global warming all in one fell swoop.

Now I don't doubt the ability of these wonder creams to conceal wrinkles. I have seen the before and after photos, and as everyone knows, such photos don't lie. I'm just not sure they truly prevent anything. Prolong the inevitable? Perhaps. *Prevent?* No.

no one ever died at the age of one hundred looking like a nineteen-year-old.

Meanwhile, the attempts to be the first woman who does have been disastrous. We've all seen the botox-injected, filler-filled, facelift–fueled celebrities who have gone down this road with unfortunate results. Let's face it: The sixty-year-old ladies trying to look thirty, don't. They look creepy. They make the clown from the Stephen King classic novel *It* afraid of clowns.

And ultimately, they're not fooling anyone. Instead, they are a sad reminder to everyone that they used to be young and are trying their damnedest to avoid getting old.

But you know what? The women who embrace who they are and own the season of life they are in are incredibly sexy.

Confidence is sexier than any cream. But confidence comes from within, not from a container or a syringe. My wife has more so-called crow's feet than most women I know who are her age. She also smiles way more than most women I know. And her smiles are actually real, not the permanent kind that comes from an overeager facelift. Our bodies age. There's nothing we can do to stop that. But the energetic childlike spirit that resides in each and every one of us? **That never gets old.**

For what it's worth, please, please, PLEASE ignore the pitches from the people who would have you believe that you aren't already beautiful.

That deep love for fun, the sparkle in your eye, the hint of mischief . . . that my dear, is

true beauty.

109

get
CURIOuS

thou shalt embrace
common knowledge

In 2011, for the first time ever, Amazon.com sold more e-books than printed books. The fascinating rise, ushered forth by mobile devices like the iPad and Kindle, was made more interesting by how the industry reacted to it. In many ways, e-books upset the apple cart, and people with businesses geared toward the old way of doing things were not happy about it.

So it was with great interest that I read an article in *Mental Floss* magazine about the advent of paperback books, and their similar assault on the status quo. In 1939, Robert de Graff introduced softcover books to America, offering them for just 25¢, while many hardcover books were selling for over $2. Even though some European publishers had success selling softcovers, New York publishers didn't think the cheap, flimsy books would translate to the American market.

They were wrong. It took just a week for de Graff to sell out of his initial hundred thousand print run, and he sold over three million in his first year. And not only did he embrace a new format, but new marketing and distribution methods as well. He sold his books in places where books weren't traditionally sold, like newsstands, drugstores, and train stations. Instead of sticking with the European tradition of stately, color-coded, and graphic-free covers, he emblazoned his covers with colorful, eye-catching drawings.

So you may be asking, "Why the history lesson on the book industry?"

The rules that don't exist are everywhere, not just in our personal lives, but in our professional lives as well. Back in the early twentieth century, the "rules" were that people would only buy books with hard covers, and they would only buy them in bookstores. Robert de Graff ignored those rules and changed the world. Netflix did the same thing when they ignored the "rules" that you had to have a physical location at which to rent out movies, and you had to charge late fees to get your customers to bring them back. Walt Disney did the same thing when he ignored the "rule" that audiences would not sit through a feature-length animation. He went ahead and made *Snow White* anyway.

Amazingly, just a few decades later, the experts asserted that audiences really wouldn't sit through a feature length movie made with computer-generated animation. Fortunately, John Lasseter and the Pixar team ignored them as they gave life to *Toy Story*.

The benefits of breaking rules that don't exist abound in the business world. Although sticking with the status quo often feels like the safe thing to do, it can also be deadly. Blockbuster could have easily done what Netflix did. But they were too entrenched in the way they'd always done things. Instead of aggressively seeking what opportunities could be unleashed by breaking old rules, they ended up being forced to close all seventeen hundred of their stores and slowly faded into extinction. Oops.

One of the advantages children have over adults is that they are not yet bogged down and limited by "common knowledge." For children, everything is on the table. They see life as a colorful kaleidoscope of possibility. As they get older, the world is all too eager to impart its "common knowledge," informing them of what's really possible, and what's really not.

In your industry, company, or organization, there are presently amazing benefits to be had if you can identify (and are willing to break) the rules that don't exist. Ignore the bad economy; take advantage of the opportunities hidden in the breaking of the rules you've been taking for granted.

The challenge is that these so-called rules do feel a lot like . . . rules. They are immovable, unshakable, and widely regarded as just the way things are done. You'll probably be ridiculed for even suggesting another way.

But the person who is wise, curious, and childlike knows there just might be a better way to sell books, rent movies, do business, or live life.

be THAT person.

OOPS

"the concept is interesting, but to earn better than a 'C,' the idea must be feasible."
—Yale professor on the conceptual paper that became FedEx, 1965

"i'm just glad it'll be clark gable who's falling on his face and not gary cooper."
—Gary Cooper turning down Gone with the Wind, 1939

"we don't like their sound, and guitar music is on the way out."
—Decca Recording Co. rejecting the Beatles, 1962

"this 'telephone' has too many shortcomings to be seriously considered as a means of communication."
—Western Union internal memo, 1876

"everything that can be invented has been invented."
—Charles H. Duell, Commissioner, U.S. Office of Patents, 1899

"it is an idle dream to imagine that automobiles will take the place of railways in the long-distance movement of passengers."
—American Road Congress, 1913

"heavier than air flying machines are impossible."
—Lord Kelvin, president, Royal Society, 1895

21

thine offspring shalt be in a million extracurricular activities

What happened to the lazy days of a child's summer vacation?

When I recall the summers of my youth, I distinctly remember my mom ignoring my brothers and me as we complained of having nothing to do. Her favorite catchphrase was, "If you're so bored, I'm sure I can find something for you to do."

Her ideas never involved a weekend jaunt to Disney World.

It was always better to languish in the sad state of boredom than to take your chances on Mom's idea of a cure.

Looking back now, my mother may have been a genius. (You're welcome, Mom.) An article in *USA Weekend* by Ann Pleshette Murphy proposed that boredom is actually a good thing for kids:

> Offering children plenty of extracurricular enrichment can be
> a good thing, but too much of it can lead to stress. In fact, 41
> percent feel stressed most or all of the time because they have
> too much to do, reports a recent poll by KidsHealth. Research
> also shows that enforcing boredom, or opportunities to daydream,
> produces brainwaves associated with creativity. When kids have a
> chance to sit with their thoughts—not while playing a video game,
> watching TV, or doing homework—their brains benefit in ways that
> enhance other kinds of learning. And being able to calm yourself
> and de-stress can have lifelong health benefits.

"Enforcing boredom?" My mom was Commissioner Gordon. But I will
grudgingly attest that the times my mom let us be bored usually led to some
exciting new initiatives. Who needs Disney World when you could transform
your backyard into the forest moon of Endor?

sadly, the lazy days of summer vacation are nearing extinction. kids are no longer given the gift of boredom.

I remember a conversation I had with my friend Randy, who worked as a
church youth minister. I asked him what the biggest issues the teens in his

community were dealing with.

"Drugs," he said.

He detailed the overwhelming prevalence of prescription drugs, and went on to tell me stories about "Skittles parties," in which everyone comes with an assortment of pills pilfered from medicine cabinets. They are thrown into a bowl, and each partygoer swallows a handful and "sees what happens." Of course this creates a conundrum if a kid overdoses or has a severe reaction, because the EMTs have no idea how to proceed with treatment, since there's no way to know what they ingested.

Heroin and cocaine have also clawed their way into the lives of the teens my friend works with, but the prescription drugs are the easy entry vehicle. Packaged in medicine bottles and dispersed by physicians, they seem safer. Vicodin, for instance, is innocently offered to fight the pain of a football injury. It doesn't take long for a habit to form. The going rate for one pill is $25. All this in a small-town community that looks more like a Rockwell painting than a crime-ravaged inner-city neighborhood.

The types of kids caught up in it are as varied as the drugs themselves. Your standard, garden variety stoners are joined by athletes, A-students, and kids involved in the choir and school plays.

After hearing all this, I asked, "So, what do you think is causing all of this?"

"Busyness," came his quick reply. "They're overscheduled and over-whelmed. There's just too much stuff. These kids are under enormous expectations to do well in academics, sports, you name it. The kids don't have time to just be . . . kids."

His diagnosis struck me as tragically simple and sadly accurate. Our children's childhoods would be vastly improved if we simply made the decision to . . . Simply. Do. Less.

And what's the goal of all these scheduled activities, anyway? To give our kids a shot at going pro? (Might as well buy a lottery ticket.) To improve their chances of getting a full-ride college scholarship? (You do know how few of those there are, right?) To turn them into superachievers so you can hum-blebrag to your friends? (Start saving money for their therapy sessions now.) To teach them the value of sportsmanship, sacrifice, and teamwork? (Aren't there cheaper, less time-consuming ways to accomplish that?)

It seems that there may be, thanks to an e-mail I received from a guy named Jay. He wrote to tell me about "Dirt League."

Finding it impossible to keep up with all the scheduled sports for his three sons, he decided summer should be about FUN, not scheduling. He rapidly found many like-minded parents and organized a weekly get-together at the park. Everyone was welcome: parents, grandparents, kids of all ages. If someone wandered by, the group would wave them in and invite them to play.

They played baseball, soccer, something called gatorball (a combination of football, soccer, and basketball), and quidditch with the help of a hula hoop and some duct tape. They also played kickball in 90-degree weather, in which you had to go through the Slip'N Slide from third to home.

Everyone brought food and drinks to share, or they just ordered pizzas. And the rules were very loose. Everyone came and went in and out of the game as they pleased. Sometimes it ended up mostly parents out on the field and the kids watching and laughing. The one major rule was: no electronic devices!

Is it just me, or does this sound like an awesome way to spend the summer?

maybe we should give our kids the gift of doing less. maybe we should bless them with boredom.

If that doesn't help matters, I'm sure my mom could find something for them to do.

thou shalt not let them see you car dancing

It's an incontrovertible fact: It is impossible to hear Journey's "Don't Stop Believin'" while driving and not transform into a head-banging, lyric-belting, steering wheel-pounding god or goddess of rock 'n' roll.

In the cozy cocoon of your humble car, you are the Alpha and Omega of Awesome.

Your inner child is running naked in the rain and you don't care who knows it.

That is until Adultitis reminds you that you are at a stoplight and there are windows in your car.

Stupid Adultitis.

It convinces us that we'll look dumb or embarrass ourselves if we let loose a little bit. And so we don't. We stay tight in our safe, comfortable little catacombs, while stress and anxiety entomb us. Rock the boat? Not me. Call attention to ourselves? Not a chance.

stupid, stupid Adultitis.

While we are buying into the rule about avoiding foolishness at all costs, we often fail to realize that our childlike outbursts might actually uplift someone and brighten their day. I don't know about you, but if I happen to catch someone summoning their inner Steve Perry, I smile.

What if instead of our traffic companions thinking we're a little loony, we were actually giving them some relief? Happiness? Hope?

My friend Ina was part of a micro-movement that invited people all over the world to send in videos of themselves car dancing. She had some provocative insights to share about her own involvement:

> *What I've found by being freer in my dance, is that it breaks down the walls between people. We live in a car society where everyone is cruising around in their own worlds, disconnected from everyone else. When you share the joy*

that comes out of you when you dance, you break through the
barrier of the car shell, and you touch someone or make them
smile and bring a human connection to their day.

Think about it: by giving yourself permission to car dance with reckless abandon, you've suddenly become an agent of social change at the wheel. You're Bono in a blue minivan, showing people it's okay to lighten up, stop taking life so seriously, and enjoy the moment. Maybe that person who pulled up next to you didn't know how they were going to pay their bills, but they saw you dancing, truly free, and in that moment, they felt relief. Or even happiness. Or perhaps the feeling that everything was going to be okay. THAT is powerful stuff!

Join me in an effort to be a little bit more willing to dance like no one else is watching—especially when people are.

Rock 'n' Roll has a long history of putting on benefit concerts to help solve big problems.

your car just became the latest venue.

thou shalt not wear thy wedding dress after thy wedding day

A wedding dress is the most expensive dress most women ever buy. And they typically only ever wear it once.

And so it was with great delight to hear a woman tell me about her tradition of wearing her wedding dress out to eat with her husband every year on their anniversary. So cool.

What a treat for the other diners, especially married ones, who are gifted with the opportunity to reflect on the happy memories from their own wedding day. And for the couples going through a rough spot in their relationship, maybe it even offers some perspective and incentive to smooth things out and steer things in the right direction.

The tuxedo I wore on my wedding day was a rental, but if it were still in my possession I'd need a giant shoehorn to put it on and the Jaws of Life to take it off. So kudos to her for being able to still show it off.

But even bigger kudos for being brave enough to break a rule that certainly doesn't exist.

{ life is short,
break the rules.
and **never**
regret anything
that makes you
smile.

– mark twain –

i̶m̶possible.

kotecki

thou shalt be realistic

"I do have dreams, but I try to keep them realistic."

No one likes to admit they don't have dreams. But no one likes to be called a fool, either. Or worse yet, a failure. After all, the bigger you dream, the more likely you are to fail. Claiming to have realistic dreams makes you sound smart. It gives the impression that you're going places, likely to succeed, and are not to be sidetracked chasing any childish, crackpot schemes. But one of those words is terribly problematic.

The word "realistic."

Who's to say what's realistic or not?

Do we really believe that Orville and Wilbur Wright were deemed "realistic" by their fellow townsfolk while they used their bicycle repair shop profits to try and build the world's first "flying machine"?

After all, in 1902 (just ONE year before the Wright Brothers' great success), Lord Kelvin—the otherwise brilliant dude who determined the correct value of absolute zero as approximately –273.15 degrees Celsius—said, "No aeroplane will ever be practically successful."

And just fifty-eight years after the Wright Brothers' breakthrough, was President John F. Kennedy being "realistic" in 1961 when he declared that America would send a man to the Moon by the end of the decade? (By the way, the first handheld pocket calculator would not be invented until five years after Kennedy's speech.)

Meanwhile, is it "realistic" today to think that we will ever find a cure for AIDS or autism or Alzheimer's disease?

When it comes to dreams, this world is suffering from a bigness deficiency. I don't think there's anybody alive who is dreaming too big. In fact, I'm not even sure it's possible. I don't need studies about how much of our brain capacity goes unused to tell me about the potential of mankind. Just look at examples. Whether it's the invention of the artificial heart, or the guy who climbed Mount Everest blind, or the inspiring examples of Holocaust survivors. We are created to do things that don't, at first glance, seem very realistic.

{ hell, there are
no rules here.
we're trying to
accomplish
something.

– thomas a. edison –

If a dream is realistic, it's not really a dream. It's a to-do.

If you want to be realistic, be realistic about your fears. After all, most of the things you worry about will never happen. But when it comes to your dreams, leave realism at home. At least at the beginning.

No matter how big you think you're dreaming, it's not big enough. A good dream has to be kind of crazy. And improbable.

"big dreams create the magic that stir men's souls to greatness." —Bill McCartney

If you're going to dream, you might as well dream big. And if you're ever accused of dreaming too big, then you can rest assured that you're on the right track. Just pretend you're a long-lost member of the Wright clan.

Don't worry about being realistic. And be very, very cautious about what you label as "impossible."

For as John Andrew Holmes wisely said, "Never tell a young person that something cannot be done. God may have been waiting centuries for somebody ignorant enough of the impossible to do that thing."

thou shalt not make a mess

I remember the day we let Lucy have full control of her ice cream cone for the very first time. It was a beautiful day. We had followed the sun down to the edge of Lake Mendota. As Kim handed her the sweet treat, Lucy gave us a look that married surprise and wonderment. Her hazel eyes shined pure joy. She licked. She smiled. She concentrated. She beamed. And she ended up with the cutest brown ice cream goatee I have ever seen. Ice cream was up her nose, on her toes, and everywhere in between.

It was hard letting go of the messy shirt, the sticky fingers, and crazy sugar buzz that would follow. But, I'm sure we made the day of at least a half dozen passersby who stopped to admire Lucy in her chocolate glory.

Kim nailed it when she reminded us both to "never let making a mess get in the way of making a memory." The shirt ultimately went to stain heaven, but the happy memory remains. This isn't to say that I don't prefer a tidy house. I feel good when the dishes are done and the counter is cleared. I'm easily disturbed when piles stay piles for too long.

Is it an Adultitis-fueled trait? Perhaps. But I do find that I am more present, relaxed, and creative when clutter and chaos is minimized. In general, I don't think it's a terrible habit to have.

However. I do find it helpful to regularly remind myself of some simple truths:

Sometimes budgets get blown and well-made plans go poof.

Sometimes grass stains are inevitable and torn jeans are unavoidable.

Sometimes eggs get broken, milk gets spilled, and the kitchen gets dusted in a fine layer of flour.

Sometimes a scaled-down replica of the Wisconsin State Fair takes over an entire bedroom for several days.

The most direct route is rarely the most scenic, and sometimes wrong turns can lead to the best discoveries.

Sometimes life doesn't go the way we planned, expected, or even hoped.

that's okay. adventures are rarely tidy.

thou shalt reserve thy fine china for special occasions

We sure are proud of our fancy dishes. Most of us keep them stored safely away in specially made furniture called china cabinets, eternally waiting for a "special occasion." Judging by how infrequently we use the stuff, it's clear that our bar for "special occasions" is set pretty high. In fact, I think we have lost all sense of what a special occasion even is. Apparently we're waiting for the Pope or the president to call us up and say, "Hey, I was gonna be in the neighborhood. Mind if I stop over for dinner?"

But what if . . .

What if you pulled out the good stuff on some random . . . Wednesday? What if you set the table with the fancy china and fresh flowers and a real tablecloth? (The kind made of actual fabric, not the kind you throw away immediately after using.) What if you turned on some jazz or classical music? What if you served drinks in wineglasses—even if the menu was only macaroni and cheese and milk?

Why not?

By the way, even if you don't have "fancy" tableware, you can still play. All you have to do is turn the lights down low and light a few candles. Instant fancy!

What this does is serve as an important message that any time you spend sharing a meal with people you love—whether it's your spouse, best friend, or family—is indeed a special occasion. More than that, it's blessed. Holy, even.

In our frantic lives, mealtime increasingly becomes just another thing to check off the list between meetings and soccer practice. And it's your family that pays the price.

When you get to the end of your life, and you're sharing favorite memories with loved ones, the Disney World vacation or the trip to the Grand Canyon will get mentioned, but most of the time will be spent recounting those simple moments around the dinner table. Traditions. Stories. Memories.

"Remember that time when . . . ?"

"Remember how you used to . . . ?"

"Remember that one story you always told . . . ?"

These are moments—memories—that you could create this very evening. Easy.

A woman came up to me after one of my speaking programs to talk about her experience cleaning out her mother's home after her passing. The woman and her siblings found a box of fine china, each piece carefully wrapped just as it was when it was gifted to their parents on their wedding day. The mother was married for over fifty years. She had four kids. Thirteen grandkids. And the china was still in the box, unused.

What good is that?

That's one story. Another one goes like this, and it was shared with me by a lady I met in Salt Lake City. She said that her mother always used the good china for weekly Sunday dinners and every holiday. Naturally, a plate or a teacup got broken here and there. But instead of lamenting over the loss, she would pick up something to replace it the next time she was at a thrift or antique store, unconcerned whether it matched her current set or not. Over the years, the original set evolved into a magnificently mismatched collection of eclectic dinnerware. Each plate, each saucer, each bowl told a different story. Not only the mysterious, unknown story of its original owner and unique history, but together they told a collective story with one unmistakable moral: Life is meant to be lived and worthy of celebration.

I don't know about you, but I like that story better.

If you're still not convinced that this Wednesday is worth celebrating, just for a moment, think of someone you love who's passed away:

a grandparent, a parent, a best friend, a spouse, a sibling, a child.

Wouldn't you give just about anything to have one more dinner with that person?

Now tell me that having dinner on a Wednesday with someone you love isn't a special occasion.

Maybe it's high time to free that fancy china.

thou shalt hide thy weirdness

One day my four-year-old daughter Lucy was skimming down the sidewalk on her kick scooter.

Normal.

She was gripping the handlebar with one hand and holding an open umbrella with the other. While wearing a bike helmet and snow boots. On a sunny, seventy-three-degree day.

Weird.

It's so weird that I'd bet anything that of the six billion plus people in the world, not one other person was doing and wearing the exact same thing at that moment. Maybe not ever or since. That's as weird as it gets.

it was also a great big life lesson.

You see, in Lucy's head, there was nothing weird about it. She was in the moment, free of pretense, and free of shame. She was living life the way it was meant to be lived.

Oh, how I wish I could be that free again.

In fact, we all were, in the beginning, when we were young. But eventually someone sees us living our bliss, decides it's weird, and shames us. We get made fun of in the schoolyard, on the bus, or across the dinner table. For the first time, it occurs to us that some of the things we do might be looked upon with contempt by another person.

From then on, we start paying attention. We start noticing what's "in" and what's not. We take heed of the things that could get us ridiculed, singled out, and shamed. And we stop doing them. We smooth out the rough edges and start hiding our weirdness. And one by one, little parts of us die.

It's quite possibly the greatest tragedy of our lives that we end up spending most of our time conforming to the world around us, all to avoid that feeling of shame ever again.

Speaker, author, self-proclaimed freak, and my friend, David Rendall, says,

"What makes us weird is what makes us wonderful." He offers up Rudolph the Red-Nosed Reindeer as a perfect example. His unusual nose was weird; the subject of ridicule and derision. But on that fateful "foggy Christmas Eve," it became an irreplaceable advantage, making him a hero.

Once in a while, you'll see an elderly person who quit buying in to the lie that our weirdness is a weakness. They're livin' *la vida loca*, carefree and without reservation. On the surface, it's easy to write them off as experiencing early stage dementia. But if you look closer, you'll see that they have all their wits about them. They've just decided it's too expensive to pay attention to what everyone else thinks, so they stopped trying to hide their weirdness.

they discovered that people only have the power to shame us if we give it to them.

Well I don't want to wait till I'm seventy to embrace that truth. I don't want to hide the best part of myself under a bushel. I want to live my life like Lucy: free, in the moment, and gloriously weird.

Won't you join me?

kotecki

28

thou shalt not bring bananas on thy fishing boat

The most unusual rule I've ever heard came from a lady in Fairbanks, Alaska. I'd asked for examples of rules that don't exist, and this woman stood up and matter-of-factly declared, "How about the one where you can't bring bananas with you on the fishing boat!"

Her delivery was as if she'd just told us that glaciers are cold and made of ice.

The blank, quizzical looks of the other attendees gave way to a roomful of raucous laughter.

Unfazed, she assured us, "But I tried it and it's totally fine."

Now, hearing about this crippling restriction for the first time and then learning that there was no reason to panic—all in the span of sixteen seconds—was as dizzying as you might imagine.

What fascinated me was that in her mind, everyone was familiar with this rule. Which is kind of how the rules work sometimes.

We all come from different backgrounds and cultures with different customs. Everyone grows up with families that do things a certain way. Often, the first time we get a clue that maybe not everyone does it the same is when we're introduced to the family of someone we're in a serious relationship with. I remember it being strange that Kim's family always ate their breakfast sausage with mustard. Meanwhile, they thought it was strange that I thought it was strange. Now I think it's strange when a waitress thinks I'm strange for asking for mustard when I order breakfast sausage.

Sometimes these rules can trick us into thinking they're universal, eternal, and ironclad, when in fact, the way you've always done it isn't necessarily the way everyone else has always done it.

Turns out this banana issue is a real thing among sport fisherman, who are notoriously superstitious and consider them bad luck. According to snopes. com, which classifies it as a legend, there is no clear reason why this rule came to be (although there are multiple possible—and hilarious—explanations). Some in the business ban anything banana related, including banana muffins, Banana Boat sunscreen, or Fruit of the Loom underwear, even though, curiously, the clothier's logo doesn't even contain a banana in it.

The good news is that this brave woman from Fairbanks confirmed that this rule is completely bogus, which means we can all breathe a sigh of relief.

And focus our attentions on not whistling on board, leaving port on Sunday, and getting virgins to pee on our nets for good luck.

thou shalt get thine inbox to zero

It seems to be the collective goal of this generation: get thine inbox to zero.

Some people become so overwhelmed with the state of their inbox that they desperately declare "E-mail Bankruptcy" and delete the entire thing with one click. We are awash in books, tips, techniques, hacks, and examples of supernatural heroes who have supposedly achieved the mythical state of (cue big, booming echo here) . . . Inbox Zero.

I don't doubt it can be done. In fact, I crave it. I've actually achieved it a few times in my life. For about thirteen seconds. But let me tell you, those thirteen seconds felt really, really good.

I just question the point of it all. It's a never-ending quest . . . is it worth it?

By the way, this rule is just a modern-day rewording of the age-old work first, play later rule, which exists in a variety of formats, such as, "Thou shalt finish thy chores before having fun" or "Thou shall make sure the dishes are done and the house is clean and the yard looks perfect before going to bed."

Different phrase, same exercise in futility.

When Kim and I were on the verge of becoming parents for the first time, we got a lot of advice. By far, the most common theme was along these lines: enjoy every moment; it all goes so fast.

Honestly, I pretty much discarded this one as obvious and irrelevant to me. I'm a professional speaker, for crying out loud; it's the same sort of advice I've dished out for years. I concluded that the givers of this advice all meant well, but clearly didn't know how I roll. I may not know a lot of things, but I knew that.

Riiiiight.

About three months into my parenting journey, I was working on tackling my to-do list, a collection of things I absolutely needed to complete that day. In a rare and miraculous turn of events, I actually finished my tasks more quickly than I thought I would. I turned to Kim, heroically offering to relieve her of the Lucy-related caregiving duties so she could take a nap, or a shower, or—*woosh!*—she was gone. In less than one nanosecond, Lucy was in my arms, a bottle appeared out of nowhere, and Kim had disappeared in a way that was reminiscent of those old Road Runner cartoons.

Lucy and I nestled into our glider, where she promptly ate several ounces and drifted off to sleep. I sat there for a few moments, soaking in the silence. I could barely believe my good fortune that she had fallen asleep so quickly. I could now check even more things off my list! Just as I was about to set her down on the couch and reach for my laptop, it hit me:

Oh my gosh. I'm doing it. I'm missing some of the best moments.

Now. I am not saying you can't try to get work done when the kids are sleeping. (That's why God invented naps!) But if you recall, I said I'd gotten everything done that I needed to get done. Here's the dirty little secret, though: There's always another e-mail to be checked. There's always someone that needs to be called back. There's always some paperwork that needs to be filed or a pile of junk mail that needs to be processed.

Here's another scary thing to consider: Every single one of us is going to die with stuff on our to-do list.

Too often, we act like the point of life is to check things off lists, to get things done, to empty our inboxes. Isn't that often how we judge if it's been a good day or not, by how much we were able to accomplish? It's as if that when we die, we will be judged poorly because we didn't reply to every e-mail.

In that moment with Lucy, that piece of advice I received from all those strangers had somehow found its way back to my stubborn, stupid, little brain.

I left my laptop where it was. As I sat there with my sleeping little angel, my mind wandered. I imagined a day twenty, or thirty, or if I'm lucky, forty years in the future, on her wedding day. I realized that when I was walking her down the aisle, or crying uncontrollably during the father-daughter dance at the reception, I'd never in a million years remember what I checked off my to-do list that day. But the images of her button nose, bald head, pursed lips, and peaceful slumber will remain with me forever.

As I write this, she's only five-years-old and I don't remember what email was so urgent that I needed to put her down to check it. But it seemed so important at the time.

And that's exactly how Adultitis works. It gets us focused on the busy, urgent, noisy things, while the most important things are happening right under our noses.

getting our inbox to zero can give us a great sense of accomplishment, but it's not the greatest thing we can accomplish.

The quest for inbox zero is a trap used by Adultitis to distract us from the things that really matter. We unwittingly turn irrelevant tasks into priorities simply because they can be checked off some list. We somehow feel guilty and unproductive if we spend too much time doing . . . nothing.

And therein lies the rub, my friend. Doing nothing isn't really doing nothing. Soaking in a quiet moment holding my baby girl while she sleeps might not be decreasing the messages in my inbox. But it's certainly not nothing.

Quite the contrary. Taking the time to be present and do nothing once in a while—especially with the people we love—is often the single most important thing we can do in an entire day. In fact, I strongly suspect that at the end of our lives, all of us will wish we would have spent a little bit more time doing nothing.

spouses shalt not swap sides of the bed

Of all the rules that don't exist, this is perhaps the one that receives the most vehement response from audiences.

Merely suggesting that this is a rule that needn't be adhered to drives as much animosity as suggesting that the Pope is not Catholic or that all chocolate should be banned.

I can say from experience as a married man that I don't remember having a conversation with my wife about what side of the bed we'd each be sleeping on, but wouldn't you know it, our assigned spots have not changed since the day we got hitched.

Weird.

I wonder what would happen if you and your sweetie switched sides for a night?

Wait, never mind. Too dangerous. The fragile balance of your relationship and the whole space-time continuum might be thrown completely out of whack.

Perhaps this is one of those rules you're better off obeying.

Or not.

{ if i'd observed
all the rules, i'd
never have got
anywhere. }

– marilyn monroe –

LIVE like someone *left* **the** gate open

kotecki

thou shalt always be careful

Once upon a time there was a girl who was raised by her grandmother in a magical forest. The old woman was always telling her to be careful, so she was. And nothing awesome ever happened to her. The end.

Parents and grandparents the world over are always warning the children they love to be careful. It is well-intentioned and comes from a deep concern for their safety.

The only problem is that being careful never contributes to an awesome story.

Children by nature are not particularly careful. I remember when my oldest daughter entered toddlerhood. Lucy cried more times in the first four weeks of walking than she did in her first seven months of life, and 95 percent of it was entirely her own doing. Curiosity is what drove her. She was always looking around, exploring, and discovering new things. In her quest to inspect every square millimeter of our home, she regularly bonked her head or fell down. Every parent knows the rhythm: first you hear a thud, a short beat of silence, and then the high-pitched screams of death that last about three-and-a-half minutes.

Shy of getting her a custom-fitted foam suit and wrapping our furniture in bubble wrap, there's not much we could do.

What's fascinating to me is that the bumps and bruises didn't deter her from her explorations. She didn't shy away from discovering something new just because she'd taken a few falls. After re-collecting herself—and getting a few healing kisses from Mom or Dad—she was back on a mission to move forward.

It's an interesting contrast to us adults. When we experience a few setbacks, we're quick to pack it in. We allow the journey to beat us. Even worse, many of us won't even start out, for fear that danger will greet us and we might fail. Get hurt. Or look stupid. Or all of the above.

so we sit on the sidelines with our safety as certain as the fact that life is passing us by.

For Lucy, the desire to see new things and make new strides was so powerful, a few knocks on the head would not keep her down. What if you became that bold again? What could you accomplish if you were a little less careful? What impact might you make on the world?

I believe we are called to be brave with our stories so others can be brave with theirs. When we live our lives as a great adventure, we give others permission to do the same.

After a speaking engagement in Scottsdale, Arizona, as I signed books for busy moms, chatted with dads, and teased little kids, I noticed an elderly woman standing quietly in the background. Once the activity level died down, she and her walker made their way over to me. "I want to share a story with you," she said eagerly.

Dorothy was her name, and she informed me matter-of-factly that she was eighty. Her wispy, silver hair framed her plump face and sparkling eyes.

"Ten years ago, a doctor told me that I was going to die," she started. "So I made a list of all the things I thought I was going to do 'some day.' One by one, I started doing them, you know, the things we always say we're going to do, like visiting someone, making a phone call, writing a letter."

One of the things Dorothy decided to do was book a flight to meet her brother for lunch. They didn't see each other very much; he never had the time and she never had the money. He took a half day off ("He never does that!") and picked her up at the airport. They had a delightful lunch with his wife and family.

"My brother is kind of a workaholic. For the life of him, he couldn't figure out why I was there," she said. "I told him, 'I'm here because I love you and I wanted to spend time with you.' By the smile on his face, it was probably the best gift I could have ever given him."

"And then I surprised my husband when I told him we were going to Hawaii," she continued. " 'What?! You're crazy!' he said. 'People like us don't go to Hawaii.'"

A year later, they were in Hawaii. (Which certainly wasn't the first or the last time a husband would be proven wrong about something.)

I could see her eyes shimmer with childlike joy as she described traveling to Italy for the opera, another lifelong dream. "It was so wonderful!" she exclaimed. "They so love their opera over there. The old theater was beautiful, so opulent—and it was even an opera I knew!"

"I had so much fun doing all of those things," Dorothy continued. "I'm sure it was one of the reasons I was cured."

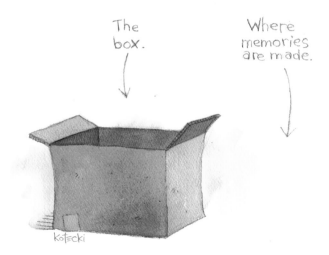

The box.

Where memories are made.

Kotecki

After hearing her story, I was more certain than ever that God intended our lives here on Earth to be more like the one Dorothy described: exciting, invigorating, and filled with moments of wondrous awe and giddy delight.

I think that when we get to heaven, it might be like returning home from a long trip. The angels and saints will crowd around us, eager to hear the tales of our life. "Who did you meet? Who captured your heart? What did you see? Wasn't the sunset over the ocean great? How impressive was that opera?" These are the questions they'll ask us, and they'll even be sincere enough to want to see all our pictures and patient enough to watch all of our home movies.

How sad would it be for them to hear you respond, "People like me don't do that sort of stuff."

Whatever is in your heart to do, do it. Write that letter. Make that call. Take that trip. Helen Keller was right when she said, "Life is either a daring adventure or nothing."

Is YOUR life a daring adventure? Or are you still waiting for the right time to take that trip or buy that dream house or make that big change?

Have you ever made a decision (of action or inaction) based on fear?

After an exercise in one of my speaking programs in which I had the participants spend some quiet time imagining a conversation with their ninety-nine-year-old self, I asked if anyone wanted to share their experience. An accountant from Milwaukee surprised me with a comment I'd never heard before.

He shared, "My ninety-nine-year-old self said, 'What am I doing here?! If I'm still here at ninety-nine, you haven't done a very good job living! You haven't taken enough risks.'"

Wow.

Common knowledge presumes that if you make it to ninety-nine, you're a success. After all, you've cheated death longer than the vast majority of people who have ever lived. And yet.

longevity means very little if your life was just one long stretch of average.

I have always loved the following declaration by Hunter S. Thompson:

"Life should not be a journey to the grave with the intention of arriving safely in a pretty and well-preserved body, but rather to skid in broadside in a cloud of smoke, thoroughly used up, totally worn out, and loudly proclaiming "Wow! What a Ride!"

The biggest challenge in my life is not figuring out how to balance my time, how to be a good father, or how to interpret what a woman really means when she says something. My biggest challenge is actually giving in to the child inside that says, "Wouldn't that be cool?" when the Adultitis in me is screaming loudly, "No, it's ridiculous, now shut up!"

"life's greatest adventure is waiting just beyond the limits of carefulness." —Michael Yaconelli

Living without risk isn't.

today, do something risky: try being uncareful.

Do something that makes your inner child jump for joy and the inner adult wickedly ticked off.

Something that just might make the angels and the saints jump for joy and your ninety-nine-year-old self smile warmly and, with a twinkling eye, say, "Way to go."

only young children and high school seniors shalt take cheesy photos near oversize numbers

You know the photos I'm talking about.

They feature three-year-olds propped up next to a three-dimensional number three and high school kids awkwardly posed in some hand(s)-touching-face configuration next to gigantic numerals representing their graduation year.

One day, my wife got the idea that it would be pretty funny if adults got pictures like that taken on their birthdays.

So she did.

And that is why she is my hero.

thou shalt not play hooky

Do you celebrate the first day of spring?

A woman at a recent speaking gig shared with me a neat family tradition that I had to pass along. She grew up in Connecticut, and every year, on the first day of spring, her father would "kidnap" his kids and play hooky. They'd all load into the car as usual, but he'd eventually take a "wrong turn," and they'd never quite make it to school. One time, he took them sledding to take advantage of a new blanket of snow on the ground. Another time they ended up at the Statue of Liberty. Since it was a weekday (and a rainy one at that), the crowds were light and they were able to ascend to the top without any waiting.

It reminds me of the dad who took his kids to the circus instead of taking them to school.

"A few years ago," he began, "when my kids were young, I said, 'C'mon, kids, we're going to the circus.' "

"We can't, Dad," the kids replied. "We have school!"

"I'm the dad. We're going."

He went on to explain what a great time they had at the circus that day. And with a dumbfounded grin, he remembered that the reaction of his kids was as if he had just handed them a million dollars.

Exactly.

Don't get me wrong. I think that a parent's first job is to model consistency and instill responsibility in their children. Setting boundaries is one of the most important jobs a parent has, as unpopular as it can often be. But it's easy for good parents to get so caught up in enforcing rules that they forget that they have the power to break them once in a while.

It's important to create scenes with your kids. And one of the best ways to do that is by breaking a rule, starting a small rebellion, and just playing hooky once in a while.

Of course, one needn't have kids, or even grandkids for that matter, in order to break a rule and create a scene. We ALL need a day to play hooky once in a while.

You can call it a mental-health day, or as my mother-in-law would say, a "sick of it" day, if that helps.

just don't call it something you should never do.

LITTLE-KNOWN FACT: During warmer months, the Statue of Liberty can often be seen holding an ice cream cone.

KOTECKI

thou shalt get a job with benefits

Many well-intentioned parents, grandparents, and teachers urge kids to get a job with good benefits.

I couldn't agree more.

Except.

Except that when most people talk about "benefits," they usually mean really, really good health insurance (with full dental!) and some sort of retirement plan that will take care of you when you're put out to pasture.

When I was going through high school, trying to decide what I wanted to do in life, I got the impression that these specific benefits were very important. Even more important than liking the actual job I was doing to obtain said benefits.

That seemed backward to me. The idea of doing a job I hated (or only kinda liked) just for the so-called benefits made shooting myself out of a cannon into a brick wall more appealing.

Fortunately, my parents did support me as I gravitated toward a career in art that pretty much assured there would be no such benefits.

It blows my mind how many people make major life decisions based almost exclusively on this narrow view of "benefits." They are willing to stay stuck in dead-end jobs that eat their soul just because they have a good vision plan. I think that a Cadillac health insurance program or generous vacation packages are fine factors to consider when hashing out the pros and cons of any potential job. But they should never be the only ones. And maybe not even the main ones.

The truth is that my job offers NONE of the benefits in the traditional sense. But that doesn't mean there aren't any. In fact, my job as an artist, author, and speaker, comes with TONS of benefits:

- The work I do makes a difference.

- I spend every day doing things I love.

- I set my own hours.

- I am rewarded for the results my hard work generates.

- I don't have to answer to clueless middle managers, corporate suits, or short-sighted shareholders.

- I get paid to travel to cool places.

- I have no dress code. (I literally wear jeans or sweatpants every day.)

- I can take time off whenever I want. (Kim and I were BOTH able to take a maternity leave when our kids were born.)

- On most days, I get to eat breakfast, lunch, and dinner with my family.

- My daily commute is seven seconds long.

Now these benefits don't come without a price. (In fact, ALL benefits come with a price of some sort.) Most of mine have required many years of hard work and persistence. Then there's the pressure of being responsible for generating income (no sales = no groceries). Also, I don't have a pension or company-matching 401k program, but I love what I do so much that I don't envision ever really retiring. Oh yeah, and I have to pay a few hundred bucks a month for health insurance.

Totally worth it.

So yes, you should definitely have a job with benefits.

just make sure they're the ones you really want.

{ the **fastest** way to **succeed** is to look as if you're playing by other people's rules, while **quietly** playing by your own. }

– michael korda –

thou shalt not wear
pajamas in public

Isn't it weird how someone can wear the equivalent of skimpy underwear at the beach without a second thought but a dude wearing flannel pajamas to Panera Bread is frowned upon?

That's totally messed up.

Methinks it's time to organize a global Pajama Run. Here's how one works:

1) Put your kids to bed. On a school night. (Yes, a school night.)

2) After about ten or fifteen minutes, grab pots and pans and wooden spoons from the kitchen, sneak down the hallway to their bedrooms, and awaken them with a cacophony of noise and gleeful squeals of "Pajama Run! Pajama Run!" (I know, I know, I have young kids.

Waking them up once you've finally gotten them down seems suicidal. But waking them up out of slumberland once a year won't kill you.)

3) Have everybody jump into the car. Still in their pajamas. (Yes, Mom and Dad, too.)

4) Drive to the nearest ice-cream place.

5) Get a sugar high. Make a memory.

A rule that doesn't exist is broken and world peace is achieved.

Extra fun can be had if you refuse to tell your kids where you're going. Imagine what's going through their minds: It's late, it's dark, they're supposed to be in bed, and they have no idea where you're taking them.

"What's going on, Mom? Where are you taking us, Dad? Is this an emergency? Is there a bomb in our house? Are you taking us to an orphanage? What did we do wrong? I'm sorry! I knew I should have cleaned my room today . . . . "

In short, they are freaking out. If that isn't worth a few ice cream cones, I don't know what is. And even more important, it's an inexpensive way to make a memory they will never forget. I've heard of people organizing school or class-wide Pajama Runs, which add the extra surprise for the children of seeing their classmates in their pajamas, too!

Please note that having actual kids is not a require-ment; it's just that kids are often a great cover for allowing adults to have fun, too. By all means, get some friends together and go crazy.

Because there's nothing better than sitting in your pj's out in public while enjoying a banana split way past your bedtime!

let's do this.

thou shalt not draw
on thy children

Adultitis was kicking our butt.

It had been exactly a month since our daughter Virginia Rose was born.
A good month, to be sure, but also a long one. Weary of the bitter cold
Wisconsin weather, our entire family was tired of being cooped up, and the
older two kids were passing time by pushing our buttons. Although we pined
for an afternoon at a Florida beach, it was decided that going out to lunch
was the best we could hope for that day.

Two-year-old Ben had a streak of purple under his nose, a colorful souvenir
from "smelling" the markers we used to keep him quiet. As I went to wipe
the marker from Ben's face in an attempt to get him presentable for public
viewing, Kim made some comment about him looking a bit like Charlie

Chaplin. Then she said, "I wish we could just draw mustaches on our kids, wouldn't that be awesome?"

"It would be," I agreed.

"Why don't we?" she wondered.

I could tell by her tone that she was kind of serious. And so I paused to ponder a serious response. "Because of what other people might think," I answered.

before I even finished the sentence, I knew what I had to do.

"Give me that purple marker," I said. After glancing to confirm it was the washable variety, I removed the cap and called Ben over. Then I knelt down and drew a bold, curly purple mustache on my son. Although he cooperated, it's fair to say he had no idea what I was doing.

"Okay." I proclaimed, snapping the cap back on. "NOW, let's go to lunch."

And we did, with our purple mustachioed son in tow.

It did garner some attention. No calls from DCFS, as Adultitis had warned. Instead, the people who noticed universally responded with smiles of delight at my oblivious son who looked like a tiny ringleader in a circus sponsored by Willy Wonka. And it was awesome.

sometimes the smallest actions are the most effective in creating great joy.

Here's a tip: If you are faced with an opportunity to do something that might be fun, and the only reason you don't is because of what someone else might think, you can be certain that Adultitis is up to no good. If you are serious about winning this war, and you are desirous of living an amazing story, you must do that very thing, without hesitation. You must.

Family with spring fever and three kids, five and under: 1, Adultitis: 0.

Being a parent is no cakewalk. But if you have young children, and you are not using the inalienable power of parenthood to draw on them, you really are missing out.

thou shalt not be ridiculous

"Don't be ridiculous!"

It's a refrain we hear again and again, and it's a rule that doesn't exist.

I'm a big fan of a web site called ridiculo.us, founded by Kyle Scheele and dedicated to the encouragement, development, and execution of ridiculous ideas. I first learned of them from their campaign to fake a marathon. That's right. People all over the world (including Kim and me) took and shared pictures of themselves stretching, running, and finishing a marathon. They were decked out in official race T-shirts and bib numbers. The only catch is that the race was 100 percent fake.

Even the most Adultitis-free among us might wonder why someone would want to fake a marathon. But maybe the real question should be, "Why not?"

Our world is starved for silliness, which is why it doesn't surprise me that the team at ridiculo.us blew by their goal on Kickstarter by over 2,000 percent or that all of the biggest viral videos on YouTube all have a thread of ridiculousness running through them. Unfortunately, silliness is in short supply.

Race cars are often required to have restrictor plates installed at the intake of an engine to limit their power. Adults are expected to have restrictor plates to limit their ridiculousness, if not banish it altogether. It's seen as a sign of maturity, intelligence, and sophistication. If you have too much ridiculousness, your taste, your smarts, and your ability to take anything seriously are all called into question.

Heaven help us if we dare to dance in the rain, make ugly cookies, or eat with strange utensils.

we are applauded for being realistic, not ridiculous.

We are supposed to fit in, not stick out. And so we make sure our clothes

always match, our cars look pretty much like everyone else's, and we paint our lives in hues of gray and beige.

But maybe it's time to reassess, because only ridiculous people would entertain the notion of writing life-changing love letters to strangers, like Hannah Brencher did when she started a movement to pen letters to those in need of a boost.

Or outrageous enough to work on fixing the foster care problem in Oklahoma, like Ben Nockels was when he founded the 111 Project. It's mission is based on the idea that if every church could recruit just one foster family from its congregation, then no child would be without a family.

Or be preposterous enough to see to it that everyone in the entire world has access to clean water, like Scott Harrison committed to when he launched Charity: Water.

Want to revolutionize the world? Rip off the restrictor plates. It's time to get ridiculous.

thou shalt make thy bed

I admit it. I debated even including this one, but it comes up again and again when I ask audiences to share rules that don't exist.

The reason for my hesitation is because, well, I make the bed. I enjoy a made bed. I like peeling back the covers after a long day and the feeling of freshness it provides. In my head, I pity those poor people who suggest that making the bed is a trivial rule that should not exist.

My wife, however, has some sort of weird medical condition that apparently renders her incapable of making the bed for any reason.

Which is why I knew I needed to include it. (Her condition also seems to hamper her ability to load the dishwasher properly, but I digress.)

There may have been a few rules in this very book that made you stop and say, "Hey! That's a perfectly fine rule! You leave that rule alone!"

And that's the point entirely.

The purpose of this book is not to tell you how to live your life. It's to make you more mindful of the choices you make and the story you're living. The rules of this book are common examples of things many people do mindlessly, without any thought or question. And that is a terrible reason to do anything, except for maybe breathing.

My goal is to help you open your eyes to the way you think and the actions you take. I want you to question.

investigate. experiment. poke. prod. play.

Decide what's best for you and do that, regardless of what anyone else might think.

So if you don't want to make the bed, I will begrudgingly admit that no evil will befall you. Sure, your mother's voice might haunt the back of your mind, but it's not like she wouldn't have anything else to hound you about, right?

And if you're one of those awesome, smart, brilliant people who like to make the bed, make thy bed. Just do it because you actually want to.

{ i believe in rules. if there weren't any rules, how could you break them? }

– leo durocher –

thou shalt care what
other people think

One time, a woman told me that when she was a kid, her mother always made sure the home was in perfect order before the family left for vacation. She suggested that "thine house shalt be clean before thou leaveth on a trip" was a rule that doesn't exist.

Now when my family is heading out of town, I also like to tidy up the house a bit because I enjoy the feeling of returning to a clean house. I imagine many people feel the same way. I was about to question this woman's rule assessment when she added, "The reason my mother wanted the house clean was in case we all died. I guess so then the people who would come into our home wouldn't think we lived in a pigsty."

Oh.

If THAT'S the reason, then yeah, it's a pretty stupid rule.

It really is amazing how many rules we subject ourselves to simply because of our concern of what other people might think.

Leadership expert and author John Maxwell's 18/40/60 Rules is spot on. He says, "When you're 18, you worry about what everybody is thinking about you. When you're 40, you don't give a darn what anybody else thinks of you. When you're 60, you realize that nobody has been thinking about you at all!"

this brings me to a story about red shoes.

When it comes to fashion, I'm pretty plain. My daily uniform is usually jeans and a T-shirt. When I speak, I gussy up the jeans and T-shirt with a sport coat. Throughout my entire life, my shoes have typically been one color (black or white or brown) with no more than one accent color. To me, fashion is all about two things: comfort, and not looking like an idiot. Since I'll never be mistaken as a New York City fashionista, the "looking like an idiot" part is avoided by keeping things plain and simple.

And then I started thinking about getting red shoes.

A while ago, I found myself in the market for new sneakers. Around that time, I began noticing people wearing red shoes. I'm talking ALL red, not white or black with a tiny splash of red. They're hard to miss, those Red Shoe People. I always thought to myself, "Man, I wish I could pull those off." Those Red Shoe People always seemed so fun and confident and full of life. Eventually, the wish become stronger and the whispers became louder.

But a voice in the back of my head chastised me, declaring that I was definitely NOT a Red Shoe Person.

"Why can't I pull them off?" I challenged back. "Why can't I wear red shoes?"

The answers I told myself were variations of the same theme:

> *They won't match anything.*

> *You'll look ridiculous.*

> *People will notice you more. And not in a good way.*

> *Who do you think you are? A celebrity? The only people who can pull crazy stuff like that are celebrities.*

> *Face it, you're just not one of those Red Shoe People.*

Eventually, these so-called reasons really started to get to me. I spent A LOT of time mulling them over in my head. It became clear that this was about more than shoes. Ultimately, I had only one person to convince—myself.

Believe me, it was not lost on me how silly it was to agonize over shoes. This was NOT a life or death decision. Eventually, I came to the conclusion: "They're shoes. Who cares what other people think? If they'll make you happy and the only reason you don't buy them is fear of what other people might think, you're a damn fool."

Well. I didn't want to be a damn fool. I wanted to be a Red Shoe Person!

And so I ordered a pair of red New Balance shoes from Zappos.

And you know what?

It was love at first lace-up. My soul jumped for joy, did an epic fist pump and executed a killer moonwalk. They are my favorite pair of shoes that I've ever worn in my whole entire life. I love how they make me feel. I'm not sure that I became any more fun or confident or full of life, but they definitely made me feel more like a person who doesn't care what people think.

"there's power in looking silly and not caring that you do." —Amy Poehler

A neat footnote to this story (Hey look! A pun!) is that the very first day I wore these shoes in public, I was at a restaurant. When the waitress came to our table, she enthusiastically remarked, "I love your shoes!"

After it dawned on me that she was talking to me (I'd never had anyone compliment me on my shoes before), I smiled and said, "Me, too."

Now. Maybe you are already a Red Shoe Person, and you read this chapter thinking, "Jeez, dude, why did it take so long to get the red shoes? It's not that big a deal." Or maybe you're someone who has no interest whatsoever in owning red shoes and secretly suspect that I may be subconsciously trying to Jedi mind trick you into buying a pair.

The moral here really has nothing to do with red shoes at all. Regardless of what camp you find yourself in, there is probably something in your life you've always (probably secretly) wanted to own, do, or be that you've talked yourself out of. You've sold yourself on the idea that you're just not "that type of person."

Guess what?

You ARE that type of person. If you want to be.

what are YOUR red shoes?

Pick
yourself

thou shalt wait for permission

Times have changed. Back in the day, a college degree pretty much guaranteed you a decent job . . . somewhere. Not anymore. Paradoxically, the opportunity to chase a dream and create an amazing life have never been better.

Not long ago, the gatekeepers ruled everything. They decided what music should be played, what books should be written, what art should be displayed, what news should be shared, what agendas should be pushed, what business ideas were valid, and what dreams should come true. You pretty much had to wait for someone to pick you, whether it was to attend their university, write for their publication, exhibit in their gallery, perform at their venue, or work for their company.

Some gatekeepers still exist, but they are not as powerful as they once were. You now have access to tools that would have made Edison's head explode. Most of them, by the way, are free. Thanks to the Internet—free at any library—and things like iTunes U and Khan Academy, you can learn anything you want to learn. With Skype, you can video conference with people anywhere in the world. You can use Kickstarter to raise money to fund that pet project or start a business. Tools abound that will help you start your writing career, publish your own books, record your own songs, sell your own products, and host your own concerts. The list goes on.

The question is no longer, "How can I make my dreams come true?" but rather, "When will I start?"

Even with all these amazing tools at our disposal, many people continue to wait for permission.

We wait for someone to offer us a job, reward us with a contract, or give us an opportunity.

We wait for someone to open the door for us, to give us their blessing, to tell us it's time.

We wait for someone else to tell us we're good enough, talented enough, or ready enough.

We wait for someone to give us permission to start.

Meanwhile, Adultitis delights in the growing ocean of unfollowed dreams.

But real life is not a schoolyard version of kickball, where you wait anxiously for someone to pick you, hoping it's sooner rather than later.

I prefer asking for forgiveness over waiting for permission.

What is your big dream? You have the tools at your fingertips. You do not need permission to become a writer or a teacher or an artist or a musician or a business owner or a world changer. You are good enough, talented enough, ready enough, kind enough, and, believe it or not, brave enough to start.

With the rest of your life ahead of you, it's tantalizing to think of all the great things that could happen.

what are **YOU** waiting for ?

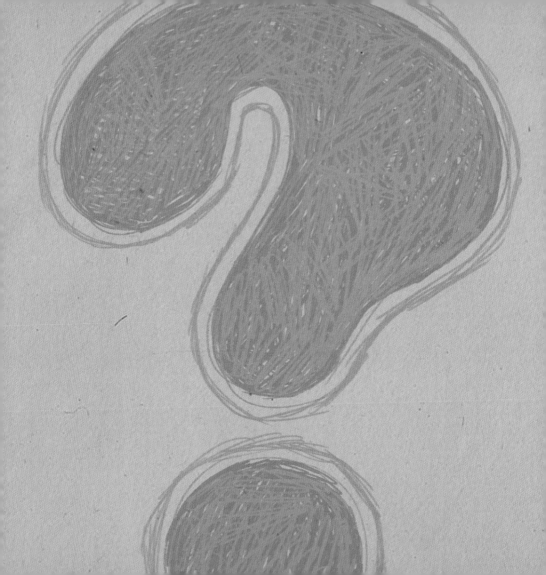

[insert rule here]

Obviously, there are way more than forty of these so-called rules.

Visit **rulesthatdontexist.com** to share

one that got missed!

final thoughts

When you buy something online, during the checkout process, there is almost always a checkbox with an invitation to receive promotional e-mails of some sort. Sometimes you have to check the box to get the e-mails. Other sites have pre-checked the box for you, automatically assuming that you want their stuff. If you don't, you physically have to uncheck the box—or opt out—yourself.

If you're not paying attention, you could end up getting a bunch of crap you didn't really want.

Living by rules that don't exist is like living life with your checkboxes pre-checked.

It's time to opt out.

Opt out of all the preconceived notions, assumptions, and stereotypes. Then mindfully choose what's best for you.

As I wrote in the beginning, this book is not big enough to hold every single rule that doesn't exist. Some are silly and easy to break, like the one about taking your picture next to oversize numbers. Others are weightier, like those that state you must have two incomes to make ends meet, live together before you get married, give birth in a hospital, and send your kids to traditional school. My best calculations suggest that there are approximately 1,385,984 of these so-called rules, although most of them have yet to be discovered. Hopefully my efforts here will serve as the starting point for you to identify the ones in your life.

As you come across them, here is a useful strategy to judge their worthiness. First, ask yourself the question, **"Why am I following this rule?"**

And then be very honest about your answer.

If the answer is something like, "Because I've tried many other options, and this is the one I like (or works) best" or "Because if I don't, there's a pretty good chance I'll end up in jail or somebody might die," then it's probably a pretty good rule to adhere to.

But if any time you answer, "Because (insert person or group of people here) has always done it this way," a ginormous red flag oughta pop up. This is a rule that could use a little poking and prodding and digging into. You have to think: Is this what I really want? What are the pros and cons of sticking with it or ignoring it? Are there any alternatives? Where did this norm come from? You might be surprised how often "the way we do things" hasn't always been the way we've done things.

Finally, if your answer has anything to do with worrying about what other people will think of you, let it go. It's a stupid and unnecessary rule that Adultitis uses to enslave you in its vile clutches.

"Why do we waste our time doing things which, if we only stopped to think about them, are just the opposite of what we were made for?" —Thomas Merton

One more thing. Please don't assume that any of this is particularly easy. It's not.

Take it from me, I should know.

I suspect that many people would presume that the guy writing a book about the rules that don't exist would be a natural-born rule breaker.

rule breaker

Three tips I'd like to give my 16-year-old self: 1) Be yourself. 2) Believe in yourself.
3) No amount of "cool guy smile" is going to offset those glasses.

But I'm not. When I was growing up, I was terrified of standing out or disappointing superiors. I did what my teachers told me. I colored inside the lines. I followed the rules. The main reason I got good grades was because I had a good short-term memory and I was good at following instructions, which frankly, is pretty much all it takes.

I never tried smoking. I never got a tattoo. I never got sent to the principal's office or burned anything down. I did try and convince my mom to let me get lines shaved into the side of my head, but she wouldn't have it. Don't get me wrong, I was not a perfect kid. I exhibited more than my fair share of jerkiness during my high school years, to which my parents will happily attest.

What I am saying is that although there are certainly people who emerge from the womb as nonconformist hell raisers, I was not one of them. And although they inspire me sometimes, there is not much I'm able to learn from them.

Most of us are not natural-born rebels. But in order to create an awesome story, you have to get reasonably good at breaking rules.

How?

practice being just brave enough.

After a speaking program in Houston a few years ago, we drove down to Galveston to spend a little time near the Gulf. As four-year-old Lucy waded in the water, immersed in a game she likes to call "tricking the waves," Kim commented on how much deeper she was willing to go compared to a few months earlier when we were in Florida.

Now, Lucy didn't go diving headfirst into the surf or anything, but she didn't need to. She was being, as I like to say, "just brave enough."

I spent a lot of my childhood being afraid. I was afraid of new experiences. Of meeting new people. Of the unknown. Of drowning. Of looking stupid. Of the future. Of being a colossal failure in life. I was afraid of thunder, and lightning, and firetrucks.

Over the years, the tide slowly turned for me, thanks to a combination of many things: A retreat that reconnected me with my faith helped me grow in confidence and courage. The gradual realization that the fear of regret was becoming more painful than the fear of trying something new. The practice of getting used to the uncertainty that comes from running one's own business. The slow progress of seeing my comfort zone grow, inch-by-inch, by practicing being just brave enough.

In the movie *We Bought a Zoo*, Matt Damon's character says, "You know, sometimes all you need is twenty seconds of insane courage. Just literally twenty

just brave enough

seconds of just embarrassing bravery. And I promise you, something great will come of it."

I don't know about you, but to me, there is great comfort in knowing we don't have to be natural-born rule breakers to live an amazing story. We don't have to be brave and courageous every minute of our lives.

Twenty seconds here and there will do.

The more you do it, the better you get. You begin seeing the benefits and feeling the freedom that comes from unshackling yourself from Adultitis, one rusty link at a time.

As I've said, my goal has never been to tell you what choices to make. I just want you to be intentional about them. Don't coast through life accepting the cookie-cutter plot put forth by other people. Don't settle for the status quo.

Living life abiding by rules that don't exist is the equivalent of signing up for an average life.

You're better than that. You are awesome and you deserve a life to match, one filled with magic and meaning and wonder and love.

Your life is a story, and a short one at that. Make it a good one.

now, go. get out there and break some rules.

Drop Jason a line at
jason@escapeadulthood.com

For a treasure trove of Adultitis-fighting tips & tools, or to learn more about bringing in Jason to speak to your organization, skedaddle on over to **escapeadulthood.com.**

ESCAPE
ADULTHOOD

jason kotecki is an artist, author, and speaker who considers himself a professional reminder-er and permission granter. He is also a husband, dad, Batman fan, Star Wars watcher, retro T-shirt wearer, and avid eater of sugar-laden cereal.

Jason and his wife, Kim (a former kindergarten teacher), are the dynamic duo behind Escape Adulthood. As partners in crime on a crusade to annihilate Adultitis, they believe that a life that embraces a childlike spirit is a life that is less stressful and way more fun. The couple inspires and encourages people to live amazing stories and make memories with the people they love.

Besides making art that inspires and delights people all over the world (all of the illustrations in this book are his), Jason is in high demand as a professional speaker. He works with all kinds of organizations, sharing real-world strategies and practical ideas for restoring balance, preventing burnout, and achieving new levels of productivity. His content-rich programs are balanced with a refreshing mix of humor and emotion, serving as the perfect antidote for people who find themselves in a personal or professional rut.

Jason lives with his family in picturesque Madison, Wisconsin, where they enjoy long walks by the lake and eat way too many cheese curds.

thou shalt go it alone

Nothing worthwhile is ever accomplished alone, and this book is no exception.

Michelle Grajkowski, thank you for reaching out, championing this project, and being such an awesome cheerleader.

Thanks to **Rose Hilliard** and the entire team at St. Martin's for believing in me and this book (and for all the hard work that went into making it great).

Thanks **Mrs. Smith** and **Mr. Dawson**, for seeing things in me I never knew were there.

Thanks **Diana Garrett, Joelyn Bednarik, David Bergsieker, Mark A. Nelson, Jay Paul Bell,** and **Ray Fredericks,** for teaching me how to be a better artist.

Thanks **Matt Tipperreiter** and **Mike and Michelle Clark**, for your support as venture capitalists in the early days.

Thanks **Pete Loveland**, for sending a lifeline when we needed it most.

Thanks **Mike Domitrz**, for sharing your bold honesty, generous friendship, and inspiring example.

Thanks **Chris Clarke-Epstein**, for serving as our wise guide and our Ahma Chris.

Thanks **Lynn Carter**, you are the behind-the-scenes rock star we couldn't do without.

Thanks, **Judy Irené**, for helping us get to the next level.

Thanks **Ryan McRae**, for being a friend worthy of The Hall of Justice.

Thanks to my brothers **Dan** and **Doug** — and the **Kotecki, Lamis, Hurt,** and **Gillham** clans — for keeping me grounded and cheering me on.

Thanks **Sue**. Your hands of service and heart of faith challenge and inspire me.

Thanks, **Jenna**. Your commitment to this cause is humbling and your friendship is a priceless gift.

Thanks **Gary and Joyce**, for raising such an awesome daughter and for breaking the rule that thine in-laws shalt be evil.

Thanks **Mom and Dad**, for giving me your blessing to chase this dream, and for supporting me in all the ups and downs along the way.

Lucy, the deep beauty of your eyes is only exceeded by the depth of your spirit.

Ben, you are my sunshine boy. Just being around you makes me happy.

Ginny, thanks for reminding me that my next big thing might be the little thing right in front of me.

Thanks, **Kim**. You are my biggest supporter and my best friend. Using words to describe how much I love you is like trying to paint a rainbow with just one color.

To **God, The Creator of All Things**, thank you for the gift of creativity, and for letting me be a part of your great story.

Thanks to everyone who has ever booked me to speak, bought something I made, sent an encouraging e-mail, championed this cause, or shared our message with a friend, I am so grateful. And to anyone I wasn't able to mention here, I will try to repay you by sharing your kind light of encouragement with as many people as I can.

thank you!

MAKE the CHOICE You'll WISH YOU HAD MADE ON YOUR LIFE'S LAST DAY.

corn kernel with combover

Peanut, with Pompadour

Fuzzy Navel

Apple with Afro

Pear with Pigtails

Pineapple with a Perm

Carrot with crew cut.

PEACE IS GODS OWN SMILE

ESCAPEADULTHOOD.COM/ART

SPHINX   BeAnie
MUMMY   Goucho
T REX/Athlete   Aviator GleAD
easter island   google eyeglasses

Are we having FUN yet?

ACT THINE Age

All progress comes from unreasonable men.

DAVID.

get curious.

AUDACITY. IS. Awesome

Hoping against hope, he Believed.

elephant john
eleraphant

key lime pie

Chocolate Shake

coo

Eat dessert first

truffles

POP STA

POP STAR

sketch book

Are we having FUN yet?

Penguins cant fly

let's get nuts

Thou shalt not wear thy wedding dress after thy wedding day.

zombies?

Without you it's a waste of time.

I just wish I'd spent more time at the office.

—nobody

EVERY DAY is a HOLIDAY

selfie

ADVENTURE! DANGER! BRAVADO!

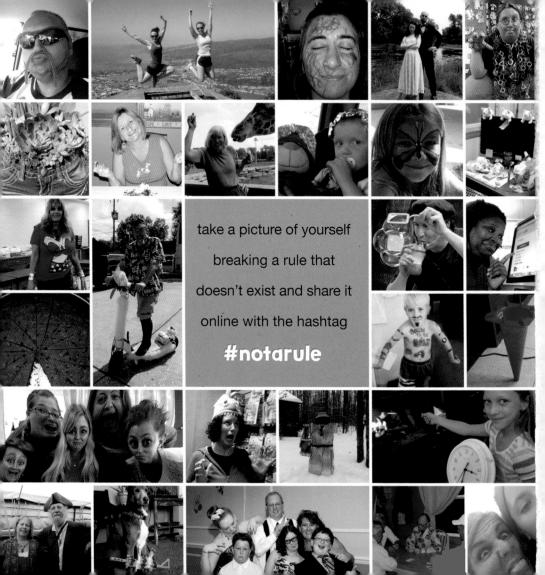

take a picture of yourself

breaking a rule that

doesn't exist and share it

online with the hashtag

#notarule